Do Community Colleges Respond to Local Needs?

Do Community Colleges Respond to Local Needs?

Evidence from California

Duane E. Leigh
Andrew M. Gill

2007

W.E. Upjohn Institute for Employment Research
Kalamazoo, Michigan

Library of Congress Cataloging-in-Publication Data

Leigh, Duane E.
  Do community colleges respond to local needs? : evidence from California / Duane
E. Leigh and Andrew M. Gill.
    p. cm.
  Includes bibliographical references and index.
  ISBN-13: 978-0-88099-327-2 (pbk. : alk. paper)
  ISBN-10: 0-88099-327-8 (pbk. : alk. paper)
  ISBN-13: 978-0-88099-328-9 (hardcover : alk. paper)
  ISBN-10: 0-88099-328-6 (hardcover : alk. paper)
  1. California Community Colleges. 2. Vocational education—California.
3. Immigrants—Employment—California. 4. Labor market—California. I. Gill,
Andrew M. (Andrew Matthew) II. Title.
  LB2361.6.C2L45 2007
  378.1'543—dc22

                              2007026908

The facts presented in this study and the observations and viewpoints expressed are
the sole responsibility of the authors. They do not necessarily represent positions of
the W.E. Upjohn Institute for Employment Research.

Cover design by Alcorn Publication Design.
Index prepared by Nancy Humphreys.
Printed in the United States of America.
Printed on recycled paper.

Contents

Tables

Acknowledgments

We gratefully acknowledge the financial support of the W.E. Upjohn Institute for Employment Research. Patrick Perry in the California Community College System Chancellor's Office kindly provided us with the student records analyzed in this project. Myra Hoffman, Willard Hom, and Charles Klein in the Chancellor's Office helped us with our understanding of the data and provided guidance on administrative details of the operation of the System. Bonnie Graybill and Carl Hedlind in California's Employment Development Department provided valuable assistance with the occupational labor demand projections used in Chapter 7. A paper based on some of the results in Chapters 5 and 6 was presented at the Second Society of Labor Economists/European Association of Labour Economists World Congress, which took place in San Francisco on June 3–5, 2005. Chris Jepsen and Steve Trejo provided us with helpful comments on that paper. We received a large number of insightful comments on the first draft of the manuscript from three outside reviewers and from Kevin Hollenbeck, our project monitor. Lu Anh Nguyen provided excellent research assistance. Allison Hewitt Colosky expeditiously handled the final steps in preparing the manuscript for publication.

1
Introduction

American community colleges are complex institutions committed to a number of different missions and to serving a variety of constituents. Historically, community colleges concentrated on two missions—supplying introductory college-level courses to students interested in transferring to a four-year college or university (the "transfer function"), and providing occupational training intended to equip program graduates with skills needed for jobs in the local labor market. Transfer and occupational training programs were typically designed for "traditional" students, namely, 18–22-year-old high school graduates attending college on a full-time basis.

Over time, community colleges have broadened their missions to include adult basic education and workforce development. Adult basic education refers to the important remediation function of providing a foundation of basic math, reading, and language skills (including English as a Second Language [ESL] programs) on which students can proceed to standard college-level academic courses or to occupational training programs. In their workforce development role, community colleges serve a key economic development function by developing training programs that assist their communities in retaining existing employers and attracting new ones. Such programs are commonly referred to as "contract training," that is, courses and programs offering occupational education or adult basic skills specifically designed for a particular employer or public agency. Contract training courses are often offered off campus at a site designated by the contracting agency.

The primary constituents of a community college are students, local employers, and local government officials. The broadening of community college missions to include workforce development has meant an expanded role for the local business community and government officials in curriculum development. This broadening of missions has also been accompanied by greater diversity within community colleges' student bodies. Community college students now include adults returning to school to sharpen their skills or earn a college degree, dislocated workers and returning homemakers seeking retraining for new careers, single mothers making the welfare-to-work transition, and high school dropouts taking advantage of a "second chance" to join mainstream society. Most of these "nontraditional" students enroll on a part-time basis as they combine employment with school. In addition, community colleges frequently serve as the point of entry for immigrants—whether they are traditional or nontraditional students—into the U.S. system of higher education.

Community colleges currently face a myriad of accountability requirements at both the state and federal levels. The basic purpose of these requirements is to gain a sense of whether, in carrying out their missions, community colleges are successfully responding to the needs of their primary constituents. But this consideration leads to a further question. The question is how to define a responsive community college in a manner that allows us to measure empirically whether a college is responsive or not.

Answering this question is not easy because there are a number of alternative ways to think about responsiveness. Fortunately, help is available in the reports of the recent U.S. Department of Education (DoED) Community College Labor Market Responsiveness Initiative. In Volume 1 of these reports, MacAllum and Yoder (2004, p. 5) suggest the following definition of labor market responsiveness: "A labor market-responsive community college delivers programs and services that align with and seek to anticipate the changing dynamics of the labor market it serves. These programs and services address the educational and workforce development needs of both employers and students as part of the college's overall contribution to the social and economic vitality of its community."

There are four aspects of this definition that we wish to highlight. First, a labor market–responsive college addresses both the educational and workforce development needs of employers and students. This means to us that colleges that emphasize remedial training as well as those that emphasize transfer programs are potentially just as labor market responsive as a college that interacts with local employers in a workforce development program that trains workers for specific jobs. In other words, what makes a college labor market responsive is that the ultimate goal of college programs is a successful labor market outcome.

Second, the DoED definition emphasizes that community colleges are primarily community-based organizations. Hence, it is important in assessing their performance to gain a sense of whether community colleges are meeting the needs of residents and employers in their local communities. Third, recognition of the dynamic nature of local labor markets suggests that responsive community colleges must look ahead to try to anticipate the needs of local students and employers.

Finally, dynamic labor markets are generated by change on both the demand side and the supply side. On the demand side, the major source of change is constantly shifting labor demand conditions brought about by changing technology and the forces of globalization. On the supply side, we suggest that the main source of change is the massive changes in number and national origin of immigrants into this country over the past 40 years.

These considerations lead us to explore two specific research questions that we believe are of contemporary policy concern:

Research Question 1: Are community colleges meeting the education and training needs of current and recent generations of immigrants?

Research Question 2: Do community colleges respond to changing demand conditions by providing occupational training programs that produce skills that are marketable in the local economy?

Two points should be made at the outset regarding these research questions. First, the two questions are not independent. Occupational skills are clearly an important educational need of current and recent generations of immigrants. At the same time, immigrants have other educational needs, such as ESL, basic skills training, and college transfer courses. Similarly, native-born students, in addition to immigrants, seek training that produces skills marketable in the local economy.

In connection with Research Question 1, the second point is that we specify education and training needs in terms of outcomes rather than access. As described in Chapter 2, the low tuition and open-door admissions policies of California community colleges, as well as their convenient locations, provide ready access to higher education. This is also true for the community college systems in most other states. Given that many students are not prepared for college-level coursework, the more important challenge facing community colleges in California and other states is to increase their effectiveness in helping students finish their programs of study. As stated recently by the chancellor of the California Community College System (CCCS), Marshall "Mark" Drummond, "[W]e have a great front door, the back door doesn't work so well" (Paddock 2006).[1]

Returning to the DoED initiative, researchers responsible for carrying out the study conducted site visits to over 33 community colleges serving 10 distinct labor market areas scattered across the nation. The objective of these site visits was to learn from community colleges viewed as labor market responsive in order to develop guidelines to help other colleges become more responsive to needs in their communities. These site visits yielded many interesting examples of how community colleges can strengthen linkages between the programs they provide and the needs of residents and employers in their communities. We discuss research outcomes of the initiative in more detail in Chapter 4.

Rather than making visits to selected community college campuses, we propose to answer our two research questions drawing on empirical results obtained from a comprehensive community college data set. Since public community colleges are often organized into statewide systems, this requires that we gain access to data supplied for all campuses in a particular state community college system. For several reasons, we choose to study data for the CCCS. These reasons are explained later in this chapter.

The next section provides justification for the statement that our two research questions are policy relevant, followed by a section that explains why we study data for California. The last section concludes with an overview of how the monograph is organized.

WHY THESE RESEARCH QUESTIONS?

Responsiveness to Meeting the Educational Needs of Immigrants

We begin by considering the very rapid recent growth in the number of immigrants into the United States. A key date is 1965, the year in which Congress passed the Immigration and Nationality Act. As described by Borjas (1987), the 1965 act made two key changes in U.S.

immigration policy: 1) it eliminated the system of national origin, race, or ancestry quotas for immigrants; and 2) it changed the emphasis in the allocation of visas toward family reunification and away from occupational preferences. Along with substantially increasing the number of immigrants, the act resulted in an important change in the geographic origin of immigrants, with more immigrants originating from Latin America and Asia and fewer immigrants from Europe.

Mosisa (2002) documents the effects of the 1965 legislation on the number and geographic distribution of immigrants. In terms of the growth in number of immigrants, he points out that between 1996 and 2000 the foreign born constituted nearly half of the net increase in the size of the entire U.S. labor force. The change in the national origin of immigrants is equally dramatic. In 1960, about 75 percent of the foreign born were European. By 2000, this percentage had dropped to about 15 percent, largely reflecting the influx of Latino and Asian immigrants. Of the top 10 leading countries of birth of the foreign-born population in 2000, 4 are Latin American (Mexico, Cuba, El Salvador, and Dominican Republic) and 5 are Asian (Philippines, India, China, Vietnam, and South Korea). Rounding out the top 10 is Canada. Mexico is by far the largest supplier of immigrants, followed by the Philippines. Over the 1996–2000 period, the foreign born represented about 83 percent and 65 percent, respectively, of the growth in the labor force of Asian Americans and Latino Americans.

What are the educational needs of these immigrants? Mosisa (2002) points out that recent immigrants are concentrated in two educational categories—those with a high level of educational attainment and those with a low level of attainment, with few immigrants falling in between. Latino immigrants are found in the low-education category. As reported by Mosisa, about 55 percent of the foreign-born Latino population age 25 years and older had less than a high school education in 2000, while only 9.5 percent had college degrees. On the other hand, Asian immigrants often possess a high level of education. In 2000, 46.5 percent of Asian immigrants had graduated from college, while only 15.4 percent had failed to complete high school.

The low level of educational attainment of Latinos—both immigrants and native born—recently received prominence in the final report of the President's Advisory Commission (2003) on Educational Excellence for Hispanic Americans. In this report, the commission notes that Latinos are now the largest minority group in the nation. At the same time, it makes the point that Latino students are far more likely to drop out of high school; if they graduate from high school, they are much less likely to earn a college degree than other population groups. Among high school graduates, Fry (2002) adds the information that while Latinos enroll in postsecondary institutions at about the same rates as other students, Latino students are much more likely to enroll in a community college as opposed to a four-year institution. In other words, Latino students appear to have roughly equal access to higher education, primarily through community colleges. But this access is not translated into transfers to four-year colleges and the earning of baccalaureate degrees.

As Mosisa indicates, however, not all immigrants are at a disadvantage in terms of educational attainment. In fact, there is currently a growing recognition of the crucial role played by immigrants and their children in preserving U.S. leadership in science and technology. A recent study by Anderson (2004) is informative. Some of the highlights of his study include the following:

- More than half of PhD engineers working in the United States are foreign-born, as are about 45 percent of mathematicians and computer scientists with PhD degrees.

- Nearly half (18 of 40) of the finalists of the Intel Science Talent Search in 2004 have parents who entered the United States on H-1B visas. Just 16 of the finalists have parents who were born in this country.

- Among the top 20 scorers of the 2004 U.S. Math Olympiad, 65 percent were the children of immigrants. Half of these 20 students were born outside the United States.

Anderson does not supply data on countries of origin for these immigrants. However, the particular individuals he describes are largely immigrants from Asian countries, including China, Taiwan, India, Vietnam, and South Korea. Also described in his article are high-achieving immigrants from a few other countries, including Russia, Romania, Hungary, and Israel.

In most states, the low tuition and open-admission policies of community colleges, coupled with their multiple locations, provide immigrants with a low-cost and convenient point of entry into the American higher-education system. One question we seek to answer is whether community colleges supply the educational services necessary for Latino and Asian immigrant students to successfully transfer to four-year colleges and universities and earn BA degrees. However, a four-year college degree is not a prerequisite for success in the U.S. labor market. With this in mind, we also explore other educational outcomes for community colleges including receipt of an AA degree and total credits earned.

Responsiveness to Meeting Employers' Skill Requirements

In recent years, a significant concern of American workers and policymakers is the loss of domestic jobs to lower-wage workers residing in other countries. This concern initially arose in the context of manufacturing jobs exiting to China and other Asian countries and, as a consequence of the North American Free Trade Agreement (NAFTA), to Mexico. More recently, the outsourcing of call center and software engineering jobs to India received prominence in the national media and the 2004 presidential campaigns of President George W. Bush and Senator John Kerry.

The rapid pace of technological change and the relentless pressure exerted by global competition means that doors to job opportunities in growing sectors of the economy are continuously opening, while job opportunities in stagnant sectors are declining. The implication for policymakers is the importance of providing an educational and training system that is targeted to real employment opportunities. At the federal level, the Bush administration's response to the issue of job losses was the president's *Jobs for the 21st Century* initiative, the focus of which is to enhance the skills of American workers. The initiative identified the nation's community colleges as the educational institutions that are to play the central role in enhancing workers' skills. Specifically, the initiative proposed $250 million in additional federal funding to community colleges that partner with local employers to provide training in high-demand skills. At the state level, in addition, legislation typically exists that explicitly directs community colleges to participate more directly in efforts to promote economic development and global competitiveness. While such legislation is quite recent in many states, Osterman and Batt (1993) describe state training initiatives that date back to the early 1960s involving the strong community college systems in North Carolina and South Carolina.

Policymakers have clearly identified community colleges as the principal institutional provider of training services to adults looking for employment or seeking to retain an existing job. But while increased attention is being directed at community colleges in their role as suppliers of adult training services, relatively little is known about how successfully they perform this function. Our Research Question 2 asks how well community colleges are doing, in a dynamic and ever-changing economy, in meeting the challenge of supplying training that meets the skill requirements of employers in local labor markets.

WHY STUDY DATA FOR CALIFORNIA?

We examine the two research questions just outlined using data for California. There are a number of reasons for focusing on California.

1. A large number of immigrants. In the context of our first research question, Mosisa (2002) points out that as of 2000, about 60 percent of foreign-born workers resided in just four states. Of these states, California has by far the largest share of immigrants (30 percent), followed by New York (12.5 percent), Florida (9.3 percent), and Texas (8.9 percent). Table 1.1 compares for fiscal year 2002 the distribution of immigrants to California and the nation as a whole by region and selected countries of birth. As might be expected, Latinos and Asians are the major categories of immigrants to both the United States and California. Latino immigrants from Mexico, the Caribbean, Central America, and South America represent about 43 percent of all immigrants to the United States and about 49 percent of immigrants to California. Among Latino immigrants, Mexicans are by far the most numerous group for the United States as a whole, at slightly over 20 percent of all immigrants. Nearly half of all Mexican immigrants chose to settle in California.

The table also shows that in 2002, Asian immigrants represent just over 32 percent of all immigrants to the United States but that they represent almost 39 percent of all immigrants to California. Leading

Table 1.1 Distributions of Immigrants to the United States and California, by Selected Countries and Regions of Birth, Fiscal Year 2002

Region and country of birth	United States		California	
	Number	Percentage	Number	Percentage
Europe	174,209	16.4	24,082	8.3
Asia (all)	342,099	32.2	112,608	38.7
China	61,282	5.8	19,494	6.7
India	71,105	6.7	18,265	6.3
Philippines	51,308	4.8	21,971	7.5
Vietnam	33,627	3.2	13,126	4.5
Africa	60,269	5.7	5,839	2.0
Mexico	219,380	20.6	105,699	36.3
Caribbean	96,489	9.1	1,325	0.5
Central America	68,979	6.5	27,143	9.3
South America	74,506	7.0	7,955	2.7
All countries	1,063,732		291,216	

SOURCE: U.S. Citizenship and Immigration Services (2002, Supplemental Table 1).

Asian countries in terms of supplying immigrants to the United States are India followed by China, the Philippines, and Vietnam, respectively. The Philippines is the leading supplier of Asian immigrants to California, followed by China, India, and Vietnam.

Just as immigrants are not geographically distributed evenly across the United States, immigrants to California tend to be clustered in particular communities. In Table 1.2, we show California Department of Finance (n.d.) data on county of residence of legal immigrants in 2000. Nearly one-third of all immigrants to California chose to live in Los Angeles County, and nearly two-thirds settled in the top-five receiving counties. These data indicate quite clearly that immigrants are concentrated in the large metropolitan areas of southern and northern California.

2. A vast state economy. A second reason for examining California data is, in the context of Research Question 2, the size of its economy. According to Rand California (2003) data, California's gross state product for 2001 was about $1.359 trillion, as compared to the U.S. gross domestic product for the same year of $10.137 trillion. This would

Table 1.2 Distribution of Legal Immigrants to California, by Top Five Receiving Counties, 2000

County	Percent of immigrants
Los Angeles	33.1
Orange	9.9
Santa Clara	8.5
San Diego	6.9
Alameda	5.4

SOURCE: California Department of Finance (n.d.).

make California, if it were considered a separate nation, about the ninth largest national economy in the world. Baldassare (2006) estimates that California is the world's eighth largest economy. Writing in the *Wall Street Journal*, Carlton (2005) suggests that California's economy is even larger—the world's sixth-largest economy.

3. The size and visibility of the CCCS. A third reason for analyzing California data is the size and national visibility of the CCCS. Today, the CCCS is made up of 72 community college districts and 109 campuses serving over 2.5 million students. These campuses are scattered throughout the state servicing local labor markets ranging from sparsely populated rural areas in the southeastern California desert and northeastern California mountains to heavily populated metropolitan areas in Los Angeles County and Orange County. The CCCS is by far the nation's largest community college system. In addition to its size, the well-known 1960 *Master Plan for Higher Education in California* has served as a catalyst for the development of community colleges in many other states.

4. Availability of data. Finally, a wealth of data is available for California community colleges. Our primary data source for examining both of our research questions is student records for the 1996 cohort of first-time freshmen (FTF) attending all CCCS campuses. These administrative data were provided us by the Chancellor's Office. We supplement FTF data with two additional data sets. The first is college-level data collected for 108 of the 109 CCCS campuses in Gill and Leigh (2004). College-level data appended to student records are used to examine our first research question. For Research Question 2, we also make use of local area occupational labor demand projections furnished, in cooperation with the Chancellor's Office, by the Labor Market Information Division (LMID) of California's Employment Development Department.

ORGANIZATION OF THE STUDY

Chapter 2 provides a brief discussion of the development of the CCCS. Included in this chapter is a summary of the main provisions of the 1960 *Master Plan*, as well as a discussion of how CCCS districts and campuses are organized, funded, and evaluated. The next two chapters provide an overview of the two distinct literatures relating to our research questions. In connection with Research Question 1, we summarize in Chapter 3 the literature examining the role of education in explaining labor market outcomes for Latino and Asian Americans. Next, we review studies using national data to estimate the effect of community colleges on overall educational attainment. The final section of the chapter discusses studies based on student records that measure the effect of attending a community college on educational outcomes for college students in general and immigrants in particular.

Chapter 4 provides an overview of the fragmented literature relating to our second research question. We begin by summarizing studies that estimate the labor market payoffs to attending a community college. Then we discuss available studies of the effectiveness of community college contract training programs and the research outputs yielded by the recent DoED Community College Labor Market Responsiveness Initiative.

Empirical results reported in Chapters 5, 6, and 7 are the heart of the study. Chapter 5 describes in detail our primary data source—the universe of FTF students enrolled at any CCCS campus during the 1996–1997 academic year. A wealth of information is available in this data set for individual students. The chapter describes the variables we construct measuring community college educational outcomes and explanatory variables, including race or ethnicity, immigration status, financial need, academic goals, progress while attending a community college, and college courses classified by the Taxonomy of Programs

(TOP) system. Since we know the college attended, we can also append to student records college-level information available from other sources.

Chapter 5 continues with documentation of gaps in community college outcome measures between Latino and white students and between Asian and white students. These gaps favor whites in comparison to Latinos, but Asians in comparison to whites. We then look for differences in student-level and college-level characteristics that might explain these ethnicity differences. We report substantial success in explaining the Latino-white gaps, but much less success in accounting for Asian-white gaps.

The analysis in Chapter 5 is carried out at the broad, or "one-digit," level of ethnicity. In Chapter 6, we exploit the more detailed, or "two-digit," information on ethnicity available in FTF data. Our success in explaining gaps in educational outcomes at the one-digit level carries over for the three disaggregated categories of Latino students. For Asian students, on the other hand, our record is mixed, depending on the particular ethnic group considered. The explanatory power of our empirical model is especially weak in terms of explaining the transfer rate of Vietnamese students, and the Vietnamese receive special attention in this chapter.

We switch gears in Chapter 7 by moving to the second of our two research questions. In this chapter, we develop and compare across colleges measures first of the supply of trained workers and next of the demand for trained workers, both classified by occupational TOP codes. Then we bring supply and demand together using an index of labor market responsiveness constructed for each individual college. Colleges are found to differ substantially in terms of their labor market responsiveness. We next seek to determine whether these differences in responsiveness can be explained by college-level and community characteristics. We find that measures of the financial capacity of colleges play a role in determining labor market responsiveness. Our main result is evidence suggesting that colleges that appear not to be particularly labor market responsive when examined in isolation may turn out to be part of community college districts that are substantially more responsive.

Chapter 8 summarizes the main results of the study and draws some implications for policy. We emphasize two main themes in this concluding chapter. One is that immigrant groups are quite different in terms of their backgrounds, aspirations, and experiences in California community colleges. Lessons learned from an analysis that takes account of these differences can be valuable in designing community college programs intended to assist immigrants. The second is that community colleges are complex institutions in terms of not only their missions but also in terms of their organization. In California, the organization of colleges into districts should be taken into account in any attempt to evaluate how successfully community colleges carry out their missions.

Note

1. Chancellor Drummond goes on to say that, "[W]e are set up to deal with the student of the '80s. The students of 2006 are not like those students. The people who come to us are not that well prepared, and there is a wider diversity" (Paddock 2006).

2
Development of the California
Community College System

California's extensive public postsecondary education system includes the University of California (UC) system, the California State
University (CSU) system, and the California Community College
System (CCCS). To place our empirical analysis in context, this chapter
provides a brief discussion of the unique role of community colleges in
the state's postsecondary education system. We begin by discussing the
well-known 1960 California *Master Plan for Higher Education*; then
we consider the organization and financing of California's community
colleges. In the next section we examine the apportionment of funds
within the system and accountability standards.[1] The final section draws
on our earlier work to briefly describe the operation of the CCCS today
(Gill and Leigh 2004).

THE 1960 *MASTER PLAN*

In a detailed study of the development of American community
colleges, Cohen and Brawer (1996) describe California as a leader in
the development of community colleges in the twentieth century and,
in many ways, a catalyst for legislation allowing the establishment of
community colleges in other states. As early as the 1930s, according to
Cohen and Brawer, 20 percent of all community colleges and one-third
of all community college students in the United States were located in
California.

During the 1950s, lawmakers in California, like those in many other
states, faced a number of difficult higher-education issues. These included huge increases in projected enrollment, rising costs for California
taxpayers, and continuing turf battles between UC campuses and the
state colleges in areas such as graduate training, research, and enrollment growth. The 1960 *Master Plan for Higher Education in California*

represented the culmination of an arduous process of negotiation involving UC campuses, state colleges, and the community colleges, as well as the legislature, the governor's office, and state agencies.[2] The outcome of these negotiations was a plan that established guidelines for the expansion and coordination of the tripartite system of higher education in California.

Key elements of the 1960 *Master Plan* (including subsequent amendments) include the following:

Differentiation of missions. The *Master Plan* clearly distinguished between the missions of the UC system, the state colleges (now the California State University system), and the community colleges. UC campuses were to offer BA, MA, PhD, and professional degrees. (Professional degrees were awarded in law, medicine, dentistry, veterinary medicine, and architecture.) The UC was designated as the state's primary academic research institution. The state colleges, in turn, were to offer BA and MA degrees and to have primary responsibility for teacher credentials. State colleges were permitted to grant doctorates only if degrees were awarded jointly with a UC campus or an independent institution. Faculty members at state colleges were limited to research consistent with the primary function of instruction.

Finally, community colleges had as their primary missions the provision of academic and occupational skills instruction for recent high school graduates and older students for the first two years of undergraduate education. In addition to these primary missions, community colleges were authorized to provide remedial instruction, English as a Second Language, and adult noncredit instruction. Recently, the legislature added workforce training designed to enhance the state's economic growth and global competitiveness to the already imposing set of missions assigned community colleges.

Universal access. The *Master Plan* reaffirmed California's long-standing commitment to the principle of universal access to higher education. This principle was implemented through low tuition and an emphasis on the transfer function. As recently as 1983, CCCS campuses charged no tuition at all. Responding to serious budget shortfalls linked to the 1982–1983 recession and the passage of Proposition 13, the CCCS began charging tuition in the fall of 1984.[3] Tuition was set at a modest

$5 per credit and capped at $50 per semester. Today, tuition is $26 per credit and tuition and fees average about $806 annually. According to the Chancellor's Office (2005), tuition and fees at community colleges in most other states are much higher, averaging between $1,500 and $3,500 per year.

Due to low tuition and its open-admission policy, California leads the nation in access to its community college system. A frequently used measure of access is participation, which is defined as student enrollment per 100,000 citizens between the ages of 18 and 44. Again according to the Chancellor's Office (2005), participation in the CCCS is 9,567 students per 100,000 citizens. This is much higher than the participation in most states, which is typically between 2,000 and 6,000 students per 100,000 citizens. Kane and Rouse (1999) also point out that California is an outlier among states in terms of the proportion of college students enrolled in a public community college.

Differentiation in admissions. Consistent with the principle of universal access, the *Master Plan* specified different admissions pools for the UC, state colleges, and community colleges. University of California campuses are to select students from among the top 12.5 percent of high school graduating classes, while CSU campuses are to select from among the top one-third of high school graduates. Separate statutes require that both the UC and CSU systems limit their enrollments and maintain specific admissions standards. To provide transfer opportunities giving community college students access to upperdivision courses, UC and CSU campuses are to maintain a ratio of lower-division to upper-division courses of 40 percent to 60 percent.

The enrollment and admissions restrictions imposed on the UC and CSU systems leave community colleges responsible for meeting the demand for postsecondary education of the remaining two-thirds of California high school graduates, as well as the adult population that would benefit from continuing education. Community college students, consequently, differ widely in terms of their academic preparation. It should be emphasized that admission to a community college is not restricted to high school graduates.

With open access and low tuition, California community colleges are more likely to enroll underrepresented groups that might not otherwise have attended college than are UC and CSU institutions.

Underrepresented student groups include individuals who are the first in their families to attend college, those working or raising a family while attending college, and those from low-income families.

In particular, community colleges serve disproportionately large shares of Latino and African American students. As shown in Table 2.1, systemwide data for 2001 indicate that about 75 percent of all white students enrolled in California public higher education institutions attended community colleges (California Postsecondary Education Commission 2006). The same statistics for Latino and African American students are 81.5 percent and 80.6 percent, respectively. On the other hand, Latinos and blacks are underrepresented in the highly selective UC system. Compared to 8.5 percent of white college students, only 4.0 percent of Latinos and 3.9 percent of blacks attended a UC institution. In sharp contrast, 16.4 percent of Asian and Filipino students attended one of the UC campuses. That is, Asian college students were nearly twice as likely as white students to be enrolled in the UC system.

Governance structure. The *Master Plan* established the Coordinating Council for Higher Education for coordinating all three higher education systems. The Coordinating Council was replaced in 1973 by the California Postsecondary Education Commission (CPEC). In addition, the *Master Plan* reaffirmed the role of the Board of Regents of the UC, and it established a Board of Trustees to oversee the CSU campuses. Community colleges are overseen by a Board of Governors that has responsibility for appointing a systemwide chancellor whose office is located in Sacramento.

ORGANIZATION OF THE CCCS

California's community colleges were originally part of the then K-14 school districts. Legislation passed in 1967 split off community college districts from K-12 districts. Each community college district is overseen by an elected board of trustees. As noted in Chapter 1, there are presently 72 community college districts in California. These range in size from the nine colleges in the massive Los Angeles Community

Table 2.1 Total Enrollment in 2001 by Race or Ethnicity in the UC, CSU, and CCCS (%)

Higher education system	Asian/ Filipino	Latino	African American	White
UC	16.4	4.0	3.9	8.5
CSU	18.3	14.5	15.5	16.7
CCCS	65.3	81.5	80.6	74.8

NOTE: About 2.2 million students are enrolled in all three systems. This breaks down to 192,000 UC students, 387,000 CSU students, and over 1.6 million CCCS students. Included in these numbers of total students, in addition to the race or ethnicity categories shown in the table, are Native Americans, nonresident aliens, "other," and no response.
SOURCE: California Postsecondary Education Commission (2006).

College District to numerous single-college districts, many of which are located in rural areas in the state.

Following the K-12 model, each community college district in California possesses considerable local autonomy. District boards set administrative policy for member colleges, manage resources across campuses in multicollege districts, and supervise in broad terms curriculum development and program offerings. Since faculty members and support personnel are heavily unionized, district boards also negotiate collective bargaining agreements. Each district maintains borrowing and taxing authority similar to that of K-12 school districts.

Murphy (2004, Chapter 2) provides an interesting description of how the organizational structures of community college districts differ between California and other states. At one extreme, states such as Minnesota and Georgia have highly centralized systems. Indeed, both of these states have gone as far as to integrate their community colleges into their respective states' university systems. At the other extreme, states like Texas and Wisconsin resemble the decentralized structure found in California, where decision-making authority is delegated to officials at the local level. Murphy notes that part of the explanation for these different organizational structures is a difference in the breadth of institutional missions. In Minnesota, for example, community colleges offer a relatively narrow range of services in comparison to those provided by California community colleges.

FUNDING THE CCCS

The state's general fund and local property taxes provide most of the funding for the California Community College System. Together, these two sources of funds accounted for over three-quarters of the resources available to the system in 2000–2002 (Murphy 2004, Chapter 2). Federal funds provided less than 4 percent of total revenue in 2000–2001, and tuition contributed only about 3 percent. California's commitment to a low-tuition policy, as discussed above, is reflected in the fact that California is the cheapest state in the nation in which to attend a community college (National Center for Education Statistics 2002, Table 168). The next cheapest state, New Mexico, is approximately twice as costly as California.

Data for 2000–2001 indicate that total state spending expressed on a per full-time equivalent student basis was $4,560 for the CCCS (Murphy 2004, Chapter 3). In contrast, per student spending for the state's other education systems is much higher. Funding available to the UC system was $22,634 per full-time equivalent student, while CSU campuses received $10,292 per full-time equivalent student. Even the K-12 system received 44 percent greater funding per student than community colleges. Compared to community colleges in other states, California community colleges also appear to be modestly funded. Data assembled by Murphy indicates that California ranked 45th out of 49 states in total revenue per full-time student.

APPORTIONMENT OF FUNDS AND ACCOUNTABILITY

There are considerable disparities in revenue per student across California's 72 community college districts. While such disparities might be expected because of differences in local property tax bases, Murphy (2004, Chapter 4) explains that most of the variation is accounted for by a centralized apportionment formula. In 1988, the state legislature introduced program-based funding (PBF) to determine the allocation of resources across community college districts. Very briefly, the PBF process begins by establishing quality standards for alternative program categories and determining the cost to provide services at those levels. Then adjustments are made for enrollment growth and changes in the cost of living in determining a district's future funding needs. Also considered in this calculation are differences in the sizes of districts and colleges. Finally, the PBF process attempts to level the playing field between wealthy and poorer districts by subtracting property taxes from each district's target allocation.

In principle, performance-based funding is a reasonable approach toward achieving two worthwhile goals: 1) supplying colleges with sufficient resources to maintain quality programs over time, and 2) achieving a measure of accountability in the use of scarce state resources. The element of accountability arises because districts are presumed to be funded at a level that enables them to meet particular performance standards. When, even with adequate resources, colleges in a district fall short of reaching that level of performance, the state is in a position to issue sanctions for underperformance.

In practice, however, PBF fell short of achieving its stated goals. A major problem is that the state failed to provide the funding necessary to reach stated performance levels. In addition, districts were not held accountable for spending allotted funds within the categories set out in the PBF formula. The consequence was that performance-based funding contributed to an inequitable distribution of resources across districts. Moreover, PBF led to an incentive structure inconsistent with the goal of maintaining high-quality services and programs.

In 1998, the state and the CCCS reached an agreement called Partnership for Excellence (PFE), designed to improve the performance of community colleges. The five performance goals laid out in the agreement include

1) a greater number of transfers to UC and CSU campuses;

2) an increased number of degrees and certificates awarded;

3) higher rates of course completion for transfer, vocational education (voc-ed), and basic skills courses;

4) greater contribution to workforce development as measured by completion of apprenticeship, advanced voc-ed, and introductory voc-ed courses; and

5) basic skills improvement as measured by number of students

completing coursework at least one level above prior basic skills courses.

The premise of PFE was that supplemental state funds above and beyond the general state apportionment would be made available to colleges that were successfully working toward these five goals. Murphy (2004, Chapter 5) concludes that, in practice, PFE funding has been distributed to districts based on full-time equivalent student enrollment instead of their performance in meeting PFE goals. In other words, PFE funds have become part of districts' funding base rather than being used as a mechanism for rewarding performance. On the positive side, the PFE program provides community colleges an additional source of much needed funding. In addition, the effort to measure success in meeting PFE goals resulted in a rich data base that can be used to study differences across districts and colleges in curriculums and programs (see, for example, Gill and Leigh [2004]).

THE CCCS TODAY

A lot can be learned about the way the CCCS looks and operates by examining the types of courses and programs offered by colleges and the type of credits completed by students. California community colleges, like community college systems in other states, offer a broad range of courses and programs to diverse groups of students. California is particularly interesting in this respect because the 1960 *Master Plan* and subsequent amendments give its community colleges a good deal of leeway in determining the mix of courses and programs they are allowed to offer. In addition, recent legislative action in California (Assembly Bill 1417) mandates that the CCCS evaluate college- and district-level performance based on standards that take into account differences in missions and the needs of local communities. As we proceed in subsequent chapters to describe community college responsiveness to local needs, it is instructive to keep in mind what it is that community colleges in California do.

In Gill and Leigh (2004), we bring together three on-line sources of quantitative data to construct 21 curriculum mix variables for each of

106 CCCS colleges. It is useful to think about these curriculum measures as they relate to three missions or goals of the system. Broadly speaking, community colleges provide 1) courses and programs that equip students to transfer to four-year colleges and universities (the transfer function), 2) voc-ed training that provides occupational skills immediately salable in the local labor market, and 3) basic skills training that provides students with skills necessary to succeed in regular academic and voc-ed college courses.

Four broad conclusions about the look and operation of California community colleges can be drawn from these data. First, it probably comes as no surprise that community colleges are heavily in the business of providing curriculums for students who wish to transfer to four-year colleges and universities. Across colleges, on average about 73 percent of total credits earned by students are transferable, and dispersion across colleges in the proportion of transferable credits is small. For instance, for most colleges in the system, at least half of the credits completed by students are in transferable programs.

Second, it is important to note that not all transfer credits are alike. Transfer credits can be earned by students in both traditional academic courses and voc-ed courses. In California community colleges, about 64 percent of all voc-ed credits earned are transferable.

Third, although most credits offered by most colleges are transferable, there are important differences between colleges in the transferable/nontransferable mix of voc-ed credits they offer. There is also substantial variation between colleges in the level at which voc-ed courses are taught.

Finally, basic skills programs are a small proportion of most community colleges' curriculum offerings, at least as measured in terms of credits. The data indicate that only 7 percent of credits completed by students are basic skills credits. In terms of the interests of entering freshmen, about 11 percent of FTF list acquisition of basic skills as a primary objective. It should be remembered, however, that basic skills services may be provided as noncredit courses.

Notes

1. In these sections we rely heavily on Murphy's (2004) useful analysis of the financing of the California Community College System.
2. Douglass (2000) goes into detail on the negotiation process leading up to the 1960 *Master Plan*.
3. Proposition 13, passed in 1978, amended the state's constitution by placing a cap on property tax rates, reducing them by an average of 57 percent. The initiative also included a less well-publicized provision requiring a two-thirds majority of both legislative houses for future increases in all state tax rates or amounts of revenue collected, including income tax rates.

3

Studies of the Effect of Community Colleges on Educational Attainment

This chapter provides an overview of the literature relating to the first research question posed in Chapter 1. To review, the question is whether community colleges are meeting the educational and training needs of current and recent generations of immigrants. Three distinct literatures are reviewed. We begin with a brief summary of the literature examining the importance of education in determining the labor market earnings of current and recent generations of Latino and Asian immigrants. The next two sections review empirical studies of the effect of community colleges on educational attainment. First we examine studies that make use of national data for community college and four-year college students. The primary objective of these studies is to estimate what are known in the literature as the community college *diversion* and *democratization* effects. In the third section we focus on studies based on student records for particular state systems of higher education. This monograph is one such study. As noted in Chapter 1, our empirical analysis is based on data for first-time freshmen (FTF) students in the California Community College System. In the last section we draw on all three of these literatures to outline an empirical framework for examining community college educational outcomes.

DETERMINANTS OF LATINO AND ASIAN EARNINGS GAPS

The Role of Education for Latinos

Influential early studies by Reimers (1983) and Borjas (1982) examine the role of differences in endowments of human capital in explaining wage differentials between Latino American and white males. Human capital endowments include education, language skills, age, and date of immigration. An important feature of both studies is the emphasis placed on nativity, and Latinos are broken down into five ethnic categories: 1) Mexicans, 2) Puerto Ricans, 3) Cubans, 4) Central and South Americans, and 5) other Latinos.

Using national data for 1976, Reimers (1983) finds that each of the five Latino groups lags behind whites in both educational attainment and wages. Differentials in average wages range from about 11 percent below whites for Cubans to about 28 percent below whites for Mexicans. The role of education and other measurable characteristics in explaining these wage differentials is found to vary across ethnic categories. For Mexicans and Cubans, the shortfall in education is the overwhelming reason for the wage gap. On the other hand, Reimers notes that integrating new immigrants into the workforce more quickly, including training in English, would particularly benefit Puerto Ricans. For Central and South Americans and "other" Latinos, differences in measured characteristics such as education and English language proficiency play a relatively small role, suggesting a bigger role for labor market discrimination. Similarly, Reimers concludes that discrimination is an important factor in explaining the lower wages of black males.

Using the same 1976 data set, Borjas (1982) also finds evidence of substantial heterogeneity among Latino Americans. He differs from Reimers, however, in his emphasis on the difference in incentives of "political refugees," as represented by Cubans, as distinct from those of "economic immigrants," as represented by Mexicans. Since political refugees face much higher costs of returning to their homelands than do economic immigrants, they have a stronger incentive to adapt rapidly to the U.S. labor market. This includes a willingness to invest in U.S. education and becoming proficient in English. Consistent with this hypothesis, Borjas reports that Cuban immigrants make significant economic progress in time periods as short as 5 to 10 years. In contrast, Mexican immigrants fail to make much progress for periods as long as 15 to 20 years. Using more recent data from the 2000 census, Lazear (2005) documents that Mexican immigrants are less fluent in English than other Latino immigrants, possess less schooling, and have lower earnings.

Given the surge in Mexican immigrants in the second half of the 1990s, it is not surprising that several more recent studies focus on the earnings gap between Mexican Americans and whites. Trejo (1997) distinguishes Mexican males by first, second, and third or higher generations of immigrants. Using Current Population Survey data for 1979 and 1989, he documents a large gap in educational attainment between Mexican Americans and non-Hispanic whites. Table 3.1 displays the gaps in education for 1989 (measured in years) across generations of male Mexican and white immigrants.

Although Mexican Americans substantially increase their education attainment between first and second generations of immigrants, an education gap of 1.9 years still remains. This gap is diminished only slightly to 1.4 years for third- or higher-generation immigrants. It is also important to note that while an average white immigrant possesses close to 2 years of postsecondary education, the average second- or third-generation Mexican American has only completed high school.

Consistent with these gaps in education, Trejo (1997) finds sizable gaps in earnings between Mexican Americans and whites for each generation for both 1979 and 1989. Even among third- or higher-generation men in 1989, Mexicans average 21 percent lower wages than whites. Trejo's analysis of the factors that underlie this wage gap indicates that fully half is attributable to lower educational attainment. Another one-quarter is attributable to Mexicans' relative youth and lack of fluency in English. It is interesting to note that in explaining a black-white wage gap of roughly the same size, Trejo finds that a deficiency in education is much less important.

While Trejo (1997) examines data for Mexican American men of all ages, Antecol and Bedard (2002, 2004) pose the same questions in analyses limited to young Mexican men and women. Used in their analysis are samples restricted to nonimmigrants drawn from the National Longitudinal Survey of Youth (NLSY). Young Mexican men and women possess, on average, about a year less of schooling than white males and females of the same age. For young men, Antecol and Bedard

Table 3.1 Gaps in Years of Education between Male Mexican and White Immigrants, by Generation of Immigrants, 1989

Generation of immigrants	Mexicans	Whites	Gap
First	8.2	13.5	−5.3
Second	11.9	13.8	−1.9
Third or higher	12.0	13.4	−1.4

SOURCE: Trejo (1997, Table 2).

(2004) find, like Trejo, that education is more important in explaining the Mexican-white wage gap than the black-white wage gap. On the other hand, lower labor force participation is more important in explaining the wage gap for blacks. For young women, Antecol and Bedard (2002) likewise report that an education deficiency is the main source of the Mexican-white wage gap, whereas lower labor force attachment is the primary cause of the black-white wage gap.

The Role of Education for Asian Americans

Chiswick (1983) investigates differences in earnings and employment of Asian men compared to white men using 1970 census data. Three categories of Asian Americans (Chinese, Japanese, and Filipino) are distinguished in the analysis, and all men in the data set are born in the United States. Chiswick finds that Chinese and Japanese men, on average, earn more than white men and possess slightly more years of schooling. On the other hand, Filipino men lag white men in both earnings and education. Controlling for differences in education, experience, marital status, and location of residence, Chiswick reports that there is little difference in the earnings of the Chinese and Japanese compared to whites. However, Filipinos lag substantially behind whites. Chiswick concludes that it is not appropriate to view Asian American as a single economically disadvantaged minority group. He emphasizes that lumping together Asians in this way hides the labor market success of the Chinese and Japanese and the lack of success of Filipinos.

Zeng and Xie (2004) expand on Chiswick's analysis using 1990 census data to compare the earnings of whites to not only native-born Asians but also to Asian immigrants educated in the United States and Asian immigrants who completed their education prior to immigration. Their census sample consists of 25–44-year-old male workers, and distinguished in their analysis are Japanese, Chinese, Asian Indians, Filipinos, Southeast Asians, and "other" Asians. The authors report that most Japanese Americans in their data set were born in the United States. In contrast, a substantial majority of Chinese and Indian Americans were born outside the United States but educated in this country. Finally, a large majority of Filipinos, Southeast Asians, and other Asians are more recent immigrants having been both born and educated outside the United States.

Table 3.2 summarizes a comparison of measures of educational attainment presented by Zeng and Xie (2004) for the three categories of Asians and for native-born whites. It is interesting to note that even for foreign-educated Asians, the category of Asians that includes the most recent immigrants, the educational statistics reported are comparable to those for whites. For example, mean years of education for foreign-educated Asians is 14.2 years as compared to 14.0 years for whites. U.S.-born Asians generally possess greater education than whites, and foreign born but U.S.-educated Asians are even more highly educated. Especially noteworthy is the nearly 40 percent of U.S.-educated Asians that have earned either a masters' degree or a PhD. The same statistic for whites is about 16 percent.

Consistent with these differences in education, Zeng and Xie (2004) observe that average annual earnings of U.S.-born and U.S.-educated Asians, respectively, are about 10 percent and 14 percent higher than average earnings of whites. Foreign-educated Asians earn, on average, about 17 percent less than whites. After controlling for differences in education, experience, English-language skills, and other personal characteristics, however, Zeng and Xie find that earnings differences between whites and U.S.-born and U.S.-educated Asians disappear, and that ethnic variation within the two Asian categories is minor. On the other hand, after controlling for human capital endowments, foreign-educated Asians earn approximately 16 percent less than whites (and the two other categories of Asians), and ethnic variation is more substantial. Specifically, foreign-educated Japanese are estimated to earn nearly 40 percent more than comparable whites, whereas foreign-educated Filipinos earn about one-third less.

Table 3.2 Differences in Educational Attainment between Native-Born Whites and U.S.-Born, U.S.-Educated, and Foreign-Educated Asians, Males Ages 25–44, 1990

Educational attainment	Whites	U.S.-born Asians	U.S.-educated Asians	Foreign-educated Asians
Mean years	14.0	15.0	16.2	14.2
MA and PhD degrees (%)	9.9	16.1	39.7	10.8

SOURCE: Zeng and Xie (2004, Table 1).

THE EFFECT OF COMMUNITY COLLEGES ON
SCHOOLING USING NATIONAL DATA

The literature just reviewed establishes the important role of differences in educational attainment in explaining earnings differentials favoring whites over Latinos and Asians over whites. Delving more deeply into the Latino-white gap in education, we noted in Chapter 1 that while Latinos are much less successful in completing BA degrees, Latinos enroll in postsecondary educational institutions to at least the same extent as members of other race or ethnicity groups. We also highlighted the important fact that Latino students are much more likely than are whites to begin their postsecondary education in a community college, as opposed to a four-year college. Thus, a Latino-white gap in educational attainment might arise for either, or both, of two reasons:

1.   A student who starts at a community college, regardless of race or ethnicity, is less likely to earn a BA degree than an otherwise equivalent student who starts at a four-year college.

2.   Among students who start at a community college, Latinos are less likely to successfully transfer to a four-year college than whites.

The first of these reasons, called the *diversion effect*, is considered in a substantial literature based largely on national data sources.[1] According to the community college critics represented in this literature, costs of transferring and a culture that places less emphasis on the bachelor's degree reduces students' aspirations to attain a BA. At the same time, community college advocates argue that because they increase access to postsecondary education, an effect known as *democratization*, community colleges have a positive effect on overall educational attainment.

A number of studies by education researchers attempt to establish the relative importance of the diversion and democratization effects. The empirical approach typically taken in these studies is to compare the estimated effects on educational attainment of starting at a community college versus starting at a four-year college. In Table 3.3, we begin with a well-known econometric study by Rouse (1995) that uses a national sample of high school seniors (the High School and Beyond data set) to estimate a structural model determining educational attainment. A primary concern in her analysis is taking account of the fact that starting at a two-year or four-year college is an important choice variable for the individual.

To estimate her structural model, Rouse uses an instrumental variables (IV) strategy with average state two- and four-year college tuition and distance from the respondent's high school to nearest two- or four-year college serving as instruments. Her results turn out to be quite sensitive to the combination of instruments used. But the main thrust of her results, as indicated in Table 3.3, is that starting at a community college, rather than at a four-year college, leads to at most one year less of schooling. Taking account of the democratization effect, which increases access, community colleges on balance substantially increase educational attainment.

Rouse's structural model specifies that the estimated effects of both two- and four-year colleges are conditional on students' desired level of schooling. However, the data set she uses in estimating her model does not include a measure of educational aspirations. In other words, her results are potentially subject to an important omitted-variable bias. Leigh and Gill (2003) estimate a similar structural model of educational attainment using data from the National Longitudinal Survey of Youth that does contain an appropriate measure of educational aspirations. Conditional on educational aspirations and holding constant a number of control variables, our results indicate, consistent with Rouse's findings, that on balance community colleges increase average years of schooling completed by an additional 0.1–0.2 of a year. Moreover, for the important case of individuals who initially aspire to complete a four-year college degree, a larger democratization effect and a smaller diversion effect increases the overall community college effect to an additional 0.4–1.0 years of schooling.

Focusing specifically on Latinos, Ganderton and Santos (1995) use High School and Beyond data for 1980 to study whether high school graduates go on to college and complete four-year college programs. Ganderton and Santos do not attempt to explicitly measure the community college diversion and democratization effects. They find, however, that Latino students who begin at a community college are less likely to earn a BA degree than those who begin at a four-year college. Nevertheless, this negative community college effect is smaller

Table 3.3 Selected Studies of the Effect of Community Colleges (CCs) on Educational Attainment Using National Data

Study	Data used	Objectives of study	Control variables	Major results
Rouse (1995)	High School and Beyond	Estimate CC diversion and democratization effects on educational attainment.	Race/ethnicity, test scores, family background, proximity to nearest CC and four-year college, and average state CC and four-year college tuition.	CCs divert some students from transferring, but effect is outweighed by increased schooling of those who otherwise would not have attended college at all.
Leigh and Gill (2003)	NLSY	Estimate CC diversion and democratization effects controlling for desired education.	Gender, race/ethnicity, ability, desired education, and family background variables.	Diversion effect estimates are sensitive to conditioning on desired schooling and are clearly dominated by democratization effect estimates.
Ganderton and Santos (1995)	High School and Beyond	Estimate determinants of college attendance and completion for Latino high school graduates.	Gender, family background, and test scores and high school GPA.	Beginning at a community college reduces probability of a BA degree for Latinos, but the effect is not as large as it is for whites and blacks.

Alfonso (2006)	Beginning Postsecondary Student Longitudinal Study of 1989–1994	Examine effects of field of study and institutional characteristics on program completion for Latinos.	Personal characteristics, family background, and part-time enrollment	Latino students are at greater risk of not completing programs because they are more likely to 1) fail to report a major, 2) enroll part-time, 3) be a first-generation college student, and 4) enroll in a large, public institution.
Gonzales and Hilmer (forthcoming)	High School and Beyond	Estimate CC diversion and democratization effects for Latinos.	Test scores, HS grades, college prep classes, family background, desired education, community characteristics, proximity to CC and four-year college, and average CC and four-year college tuition.	Estimated effects are sensitive to estimation technique. Nevertheless, both OLS and IV estimates indicate that democratization exceeds diversion for Latinos.
Leigh and Gill (2004)	NLSY	Estimate CC diversion and democratization effects using change in educational aspirations.	Gender, race/ethnicity, ability, desired education, and family background variables.	CC effect on expanding educational aspirations is sizable. This is especially the case for students from economically disadvantaged backgrounds, such as Latinos.

for Latinos than it is for whites and blacks. Three of their other findings should be briefly mentioned. First, foreign-born Latinos are more likely to attend college than U.S.-born Latinos. Second, other things equal, Mexicans are less likely to graduate with a BA degree than are other Latino students. Finally, in addition to the negative effect of starting at a community college, the lower probability of earning a BA degree for Latinos compared to whites is explained by factors including lower family socioeconomic status, delayed entry into college after high school, and a greater likelihood of attending college part time.

Alfonso (2006) begins from the premise that much of the diversion effect/democratization effect debate ignores students in occupational programs and those pursuing certificates rather than degrees. Using nationally representative data from the Beginning Postsecondary Student Longitudinal Study of 1989–1994, she examines two outcomes: completion of certificates for students who initially indicate an interest in occupational training, and completion of an AA degree (and/or transferring) for those interested in ultimately earning a degree. Students included in the data set include those enrolled in public vocational or trade schools and private technical institutions, in addition to community colleges.

Focusing on Latinos, Alfonso (2006) reports the rather surprising conclusion that Latino students do about as well as whites, other things equal, in terms of completing their programs. Nevertheless, she finds that Latinos have personal characteristics that put them at greater risk of not completing. These characteristics include 1) a lower probability of reporting a major upon initial enrollment, 2) a greater likelihood of working and attending college part time, and 3) a greater probability of being a first-generation college student. Note the overlap between these characteristics and those pointed to by Ganderton and Santos (1995). In addition, Alfonso emphasizes the difference between Latinos and other students in the type and size of postsecondary institutions attended. Specifically, Latinos are less likely than other students to enroll in private institutions and more likely to enroll in large public community colleges.

Continuing this concentration on Latinos, Gonzalez and Hilmer (forthcoming) apply Rouse's model, as amended by Leigh and Gill (2003), to the question of whether diversion and democratization effects estimated for Latino community college students differ from those estimated for whites. That is, the authors consider the second of the two reasons for a Latino-white gap in educational attainment mentioned at the beginning of this section. Using High School and Beyond data, Gonzales and Hilmer present both OLS and IV estimates of diversion and democratization effects for Latino, white, and black students. For each race or ethnicity category, their IV estimates are substantially larger than corresponding OLS estimates, suggesting a need for caution in interpreting their results. Nevertheless, the main message of their analysis is that the community college democratization effect dominates the diversion effect for Latinos. This is not the case for white and black students.

One last study presents an alternative approach to testing the community college diversion hypothesis. Rather than focusing on educational attainment, Kane and Rouse (1999) suggest looking at whether changes in educational aspirations that occur after students enter college are related to the type of college attended. To carry out this proposed test, Leigh and Gill (2004) use information on educational aspirations measured in two different years available in the NLSY data set. Controlling for desired schooling in the initial period, our results indicate that, contrary to the diversion effect, community colleges substantially expand the educational aspirations of their students. Moreover, we find that enhanced educational aspirations are especially large for students from disadvantaged backgrounds, which we define empirically as 1) neither parent attended college, 2) family income less than $10,000, 3) blacks, and 4) Latinos.

THE EFFECT OF COMMUNITY COLLEGES ON SCHOOLING USING STUDENT RECORDS

At the beginning of the previous section, we introduced two reasons why Latino students, who disproportionately enroll in community colleges, are less likely to earn BA degrees than comparable whites. We examined the first reason, which applies regardless of a student's race or ethnicity, in the context of the community college diversion effect literature. The second reason raises the possibility that Latino community college students are less likely to successfully transfer to a four-year college than other community college students. All of the studies reviewed, and summarized in Table 3.3, are based on national data.

There is also a substantial literature using data for particular state higher-education systems that examines differences in educational outcomes, including transfers to four-year colleges, for students who begin their college careers at a community college. Five of these studies are summarized in Table 3.4. Note that all of the studies utilize student records for state higher-education systems in either California or New York.

The first study, by Ehrenberg and Smith (2004), uses grouped data for students who transferred between the 36 community colleges and colleges of technology and the 19 four-year institutions in the State University of New York (SUNY) system. The Ehrenberg-Smith data set includes information on whether students in a group earned an AA degree before transferring and, if they transferred, whether they completed a BA degree, were still enrolled at the four-year institution, or had dropped out of the four-year institution. Since they can identify particular two-year and four-year colleges, the authors are able to examine the performance of each community college in preparing its students to successfully transfer and complete a four-year college program.

Using their grouped data, Ehrenberg and Smith (2004) find that estimated effects for many two-year colleges are insignificantly different from zero, meaning that the impact on earning a BA degree of having transferred from these institutions cannot be distinguished from that of having transferred from an arbitrarily chosen reference institution. Nevertheless, quite large effects are found for a handful of community colleges. Specifically, estimated graduation rates range from as high as 23 percentage points above that of the reference community college to as low as 33 percentage points below that of the reference community college. Ehrenberg and Smith also show that these differences in estimated effects largely disappear once student preparation and backgrounds, as measured by two-year degrees and four-year college freshman graduation rates, are controlled for in the analysis.

One final point of interest in the Ehrenberg and Smith (2004) study is the authors' recommendation that further research be carried out using individual student records. As they suggest, such data would identify students' gender, race or ethnicity, financial background, and credit hours prior to transferring; and these individual-level variables could be coupled as control variables with institution-specific variables. As will be discussed in Chapter 5, we are able to follow up on this recommendation since we have information for individual students attending California Community College System (CCCS) campuses, and we can link campus-level information to these student-level data.[2] Since CCCS data are specific to community college students, we are not, however, able to connect information for two- and four-year colleges to measure success in completing four-year college programs.

The next two studies described in Table 3.4 use California community college data. The objective of the Chancellor's Office (2002) study is to develop a statistical model that predicts "expected" transfer rates for each CCCS campus on the basis of factors largely out of its control. Then actual and expected transfer rates can be compared to identify those community colleges with persistently low transfer rates. The statistical model includes as explanatory variables the academic ability of the college's entering students as measured by the Academic Preparation Index (API), proportion of students over age 25, proximity to nearest California State University (CSU) campus, and county measures of income and unemployment. Of these variables, statistically significant effects are found for the API, student age, and CSU proximity. About 70 percent of community colleges report an actual transfer rate that is reasonably close to the expected rate—that is, within plus or minus 5 percentage points of the predicted rate. Eighteen community colleges are found to have positive residuals that exceed 5.0 percentage points, while another 14 colleges have negative residuals bigger than 5.0 percentage points in absolute value.

The Chancellor's Office model does not include measures of the race or ethnicity mixes of each campus. Wassmer, Moore, and Shulock (2004) add race/ethnicity variables to the model to investigate the nature of barriers faced by minority groups underrepresented among baccalaureate degree recipients. The authors point out that in California the percentages of community college students who are Asian American and Latino have more than doubled in the past 20 years, while the share that is African American has remained fairly constant. At the same time, Latino and African American students are underrepresented, in comparison to their shares of total enrollment, in the percentage of students that successfully transfers to California's four-year institutions. Asians, in contrast, are overrepresented among transferring students.

Table 3.4 Selected Studies of the Effect of Community Colleges (CCs) on Educational Attainment Using State Administrative Data

Study	Data used	Objectives of study	Explanatory variables	Major results
Ehrenberg and Smith (2004)	Grouped data for CCs and four-year colleges in the SUNY system.	Assess CC performance in preparing students to transfer and complete BA degrees.	AA degree, distance between CC and four-year college, county average earnings and unemployment rate, and college graduation rate and admissions standards.	Sizable differences between CCs in students' success in graduating from SUNY four-year colleges. But estimates are sensitive to measures of student preparedness.
Chancellor's Office (2002)	College-level data for the 1993–99 cohort of first-time freshmen seeking degrees for all California CCs.	Identify colleges with persistently low transfer rates.	College API, students age 25+, county per-capita income and unemployment rate, and proximity to CSU campus.	API is particularly strong indicator of transfer rates. Most colleges are within five points in either direction of predicted transfer rate.
Wassmer, Moore, and Shulock (2004)	College-level data for first-time freshmen cohorts at California CCs.	Identify factors, including race and ethnicity, that explain observed differences in transfer rates.	Same as Chancellor's Office (2002), with the addition of race/ethnicity measures and student interest in transferring and fraction of liberal arts degrees.	A modest positive effect on transfer rates of share of Asian students (relative to whites). Some evidence of a negative effect for share of Latinos.

Bailey and Weininger (2002)	Individual students in fall 1990 cohort of first-time freshmen entering CUNY CCs.	Assess the educational experiences of foreign-born graduates of foreign and U.S. high schools.	BA aspirations, employment status, family background, test scores, race/ethnicity, and foreign/domestic high school.	Foreign-born students, in comparison to natives, earn more credits, are more likely to earn an AA, and are at least as likely to transfer. Controlling for nativity, no effect of race/ethnicity except on likelihood of earning BA.
Leinbach and Bailey (2006)	1990 CUNY first-time freshman who provided race/ethnicity and nativity information.	Assess the access and performance of native- and foreign-born Latinos to comparable non-Latinos.	Gender, age, family background, working part- or full-time, test scores, BA aspirations, initial program and institution.	Performance of foreign-born students generally exceeds that of natives. However, this is not the case for Latinos.

In addition to race or ethnicity, Wassmer, Moore, and Shulock (2004) augment the variables in the Chancellor's Office (2002) model with measures at the college level of students' interest in transferring and proportion of degrees awarded in general studies or liberal arts. Controlling for these variables, they report a negative effect on transfer rates measured over the 1994–1997 period of the share of Latino students as well as the share of African American students. Transfer rates are measured over a period of three years, over a six-year period, and over six years for students "intending to transfer." There is also evidence that the share of Asian students increases transfer rates.

In discussing these results, Wassmer, Moore, and Shulock (2004) speculate on the possible importance of a variety of student-specific and campus-specific factors that might underlie estimated race or ethnicity effects. These factors include part-time employment, enrollment at an older age, discontinuous enrollment, insufficient financial aid, lack of mentoring and peer support, and attendance at colleges lacking an effective "transfer culture."[3] The authors also provide an interesting discussion of what is known as "Hispanic culture." They suggest that while individual Latino parents value the education of their children, the broader culture places a higher value on family welfare than on individual aspirations and encourages Latino youth to remain close to home and family. The need to stay close to home and to contribute financially to the family makes it difficult for Latino students to transfer to four-year colleges, which may not be located nearby or may not offer flexible class schedules compatible with holding a job while attending school.

In contrast, what is usually meant by "Asian culture" is the belief held by Asian families that education is the primary mechanism for getting ahead in American society. This belief is often asserted to be particularly strongly held by first-generation immigrant parents. Asian children are consequently encouraged to work hard and excel in their academic studies. For their part, parents exhibit a willingness to make sacrifices financially to be sure that their children have all the resources they need to do well in school.[4]

Wassmer, Moore, and Shulock (2004) conclude by noting that in view of the large and growing Latino population in California, more research is needed to understand the barriers faced by Latino students to a successful transfer experience. To make progress in this research effort, they, like Ehrenberg and Smith (2003), recommend the use of student-specific data in order to explore in greater detail the relationship between student characteristics and transfer behavior.

The final two studies summarized in Table 3.4 use individual-level data for students enrolled in two- and four-year colleges in the City University of New York (CUNY) system. Motivating the study by Bailey and Weininger (2002) is the enrollment pressure exerted on CUNY's community colleges by two factors: the huge influx of immigrants into New York City, and the recommendation of a 1999 Mayor's Task Force that two-year colleges be solely responsible for providing remediation services. Since immigrants are frequently in need of remedial education, especially training in English language skills, these two factors are directly related.

Focusing on immigrants, Bailey and Weininger (2002) examine the choice between attending a two-year or four-year CUNY college or university and the effect of this choice on educational outcomes. Their analysis is largely based on data for 8,332 FTF students who provided information on their places of birth. Descriptive statistics indicate that whites and Asians—whether native or foreign born—are more likely to begin in four-year colleges, while African Americans and Latinos are more likely to initially enroll in a community college. Their regression analysis indicates that the concentration of Latinos in community colleges can be largely explained by low assessment test scores. Similarly, the Asian overrepresentation in four-year colleges can be substantially explained by a superior educational background.

CUNY data permit measurement of several educational outcomes for community college students. These include 1) number of credits earned, whether earned in a two-year or four-year college; 2) receipt of an AA degree; 3) transfer to a four-year college; and 4) transferring and earning a BA degree. In analyzing the determinants of these outcomes, Bailey and Weininger (2002) control for an impressive variety of student and family characteristics, including student educational aspirations and test scores. However, they do not otherwise attempt to take into account the endogeneity of the initial choice between enrolling in a two-year or four-year college. Their regression results indicate that foreign-born students, in comparison to natives, earn more credits, are more likely to transfer, are more likely to receive an AA degree, and, after transferring, are more likely to earn a BA degree. Once nativity has been taken into account, the effects of race or ethnicity tend to be small and are frequently statistically insignificant. The exception to this statement is that, regardless of nativity, African American and Latino students who transfer are much less likely than white and Asian students to graduate with a BA.

In a follow-up study, Leinbach and Bailey (2006) conduct a separate analysis for Latino students enrolled in the CUNY system. As noted in the earlier study by Bailey and Weininger, Latino students are concentrated in community colleges. Compared to non-Latinos, Leinbach and Bailey find that Latino students earn fewer total credits and are less likely to receive a BA degree. Smaller differences between Latinos and non-Latinos are observed for receipt of an AA degree and probability of transferring.

Stratifying students by immigrant status, furthermore, Leinbach and Bailey (2006) report two additional findings distinguishing foreign-born Latinos from other native and foreign-born groups. First, foreign-born Latinos earn significantly fewer credits compared with other immigrants, and this difference is found to be far larger than the difference between native-born Latinos and other native-born groups. Latino immigrants also have a very low rate of bachelor's degree attainment relative to other groups. Second, explanatory variables including initial enrollment in a community college or a four-year college, test scores, and possession of a GED do not seem to affect educational outcomes for Latinos, whereas they are significant determinants of outcome variables for other CUNY students.

Leinbach and Bailey (2006) emphasize that the relatively poor performance of foreign-born Latinos in comparison to other foreign-born students is an important and disturbing finding. They suggest that useful areas of further research should include the possibilities that 1) the educational aspirations of Latino immigrants are different from those of other immigrants, 2) Latino immigrants have different reasons for coming to New York City, and 3) there are important cultural differences between Latinos and other immigrant populations.

A FRAMEWORK FOR EXAMINING COMMUNITY
COLLEGE EDUCATIONAL OUTCOMES

The three literatures reviewed in this chapter offer guidance for our empirical analysis of the question of whether community colleges are meeting the educational needs of current and recent generations of immigrants. As discussed in the first section of this chapter, the literature examining differentials in earnings between Latinos and whites and Asians and whites makes it clear that differences in educational endowments are consistently found to be an important factor in explaining earnings differentials. At the same time, workers of different national origins within the broad Latino and Asians categories appear to differ substantially in their endowments of education and in the possible importance of educational endowments in explaining labor market outcomes. This literature makes it clear we need to make the greatest use possible of detail available for Latino and Asian American students on their national origins.

Focusing on the determinants of educational attainment, the literature discussed in the second section uses nationally representative data to estimate community college diversion and democratization effects, controlling for a number of explanatory variables. Drawing on this literature, key explanatory variables measured for individual students that should be considered in our analysis include

- student preparation and background,

- financial need,

- academic ability, and

- interest in an academic curriculum laying the groundwork for transferring to a four-year college, as opposed to an interest in an occupational skills program.

Finally, the third section describes a literature that draws on student records available for state higher-education systems to estimate the effect of attending a community college on educational attainment. This literature suggests two final guidelines for our analysis. The first is that useful community college outcome variables include

- transferring to a four-year college,

- receipt of an AA degree, and
- total number of credits earned.

Each of these outcome variables captures a somewhat different aspect of educational attainment. Since a four-year-college degree requires that a community college student first transfer, the initial outcome directly relates to the usual measure of educational attainment, namely, years of education completed. Associate's degree holders include students who transfer intending to earn a bachelor's degree as well as students for whom the AA is a final degree. For students who enter the labor market immediately following their community college experience, studies such as Kane and Rouse (1995) and Leigh and Gill (1997) show that receipt of an AA degree generates a sizable premium compared to the earnings of high school graduates with no postsecondary education. Finally, a measure of total credits earned addresses the important point made by Kane and Rouse (1995) that many community college students complete very few credits during their college careers. A sizable number of credits earned reflect an investment large enough to be meaningful in terms of successfully transferring to a four-year college or competing effectively in the labor market.

The second guideline recognizes that even after controlling for a variety of student-level explanatory variables, substantial differences in outcome variables may still exist across individual campuses. This suggests that if community college attended can be identified, careful attention should be paid to differences between colleges in their "transfer culture" and other institution-specific characteristics.

Expounding on the studies based on student records discussed in the third section, Chapter 5 describes the data set for California community college students we use in our empirical analysis. Strengths of our data include, for a large number of students, a wealth of information on student characteristics and community college outcome variables. Student characteristics include college attended and detailed data on race or ethnicity. The information on college attended allows us to match institution-specific information with the data available for each student. A weakness of our data set is that information is not collected for family background variables such as family income and parents' education. This is a limitation in terms of measuring the financial need of students. In Chapters 5 and 6, we report the results of our analysis.

Chapter 5 documents Latino-white and Asian-white gaps in our community college outcome variables, and suggests possible differences between Latinos, Asians, and whites in student attributes and college characteristics that might account for these gaps. Our analysis in this chapter is at the broad, or "one-digit," breakdown of race or ethnicity. Chapter 6 reports on our success, now using the more detailed or "two-digit" ethnicity breakdown available for Latinos and Asians, of using the same extensive list of student-level and college-level explanatory variables in explaining observed gaps in educational outcomes.

Notes

1. Kane and Rouse (1999) and Leigh and Gill (2003) provide a useful overview of this literature.
2. In a study discussed in Chapter 5, Bailey et al. (2005) link institution-specific data from the Integrated Postsecondary Education Data System to student-level data from the National Education Longitudinal Study of 1988. While they use a national data set in their study, the authors suggest that future research be based on state-level student records that offer the advantages of 1) much larger samples and 2) significant numbers of students within individual community colleges.
3. Note the connection between emphasis on lack of a transfer culture and the argument in the diversion effect literature that attending a community college may suppress students' aspirations to attain a BA degree.
4. Writing in the *Wall Street Journal*, Hwang (2005) describes the Asian culture existing at two public high schools with outstanding academic reputations located in the cities of Cupertino and San Jose in the Silicon Valley region of Northern California. Both high schools have a large and growing proportion of Asian students. The article brings out clearly the pressures on children to excel in school exerted particularly by Asian parents who are first-generation immigrants. The intense academic competition that results, according to Hwang, has led white parents and even other Asian parents to find alternative public or private high schools with less competitive pressure—and fewer Asian students.

4

Studies of Community Colleges' Responsiveness to Changes in Employer Skill Requirements

In Chapter 1 we advanced a definition of labor market responsiveness borrowed from the recent U.S. Department of Education (DoED) Community College Labor Market Responsiveness Initiative. An important aspect of this definition is that a labor market responsive community college seeks to develop programs that are aligned to changes on both the demand and supply side of its local labor market. Based on the DoED definition, we posed two research questions that we propose to answer using California community college data. Literature related to the first question, which concerns important supply-side change associated with immigration, was reviewed in Chapter 3. The second question asked whether community colleges respond to changing demand conditions by providing occupational training programs that produce skills marketable in the local economy.

Economists use the term *labor market efficiency* to refer to the speed with which individuals seeking employment are matched to vacant jobs in local labor markets. To provide some background for our consideration of Research Question 2, we review in this chapter a fragmented literature that looks at the role of community colleges in increasing labor market efficiency by putting in place training curriculums responsive to local employer needs. The first three entries of Table 4.1 provide an overview of the primary approaches taken in this literature.

Drawing on this table, we begin by examining the empirical literature measuring the impact of community college training programs on labor market outcomes. In the second section we consider qualitative and some quantitative results from the DoED Community College Labor Market Responsiveness Initiative. We then give an overview of a small number of studies examining contract training, typically the most direct form of outreach by community colleges to local employers. We conclude by outlining a new empirically based approach to measuring,

48

Table 4.1 Overview of Alternative Approaches to Assessing the Impact of Community Colleges (CCs) on Labor Market Efficiency

Approach	Studies	Key features	Outcome
Estimate labor market effects of alternative CC fields of study.	Leigh and Gill (2001); Jacobson, LaLonde, and Sullivan (2005a,b).	Estimates are available from national data, but preferred estimates come from state administrative data matching CC student records with UI wage histories.	Enrollment in a CC has a positive impact on earnings, with earnings estimates varying substantially across fields of study.
Site visits to learn what CCs can do to become more responsive to local labor market needs.	DoED Community College Labor Market Responsiveness Initiative (MacAllum and Yoder 2004).	Information obtained from visiting over 30 CCs, including four in California.	"Best practice" examples and two survey instruments intended to provide guidance to college administrators seeking greater labor market responsiveness.
Studies of the incidence and effectiveness of CC contract training.	Dougherty (2003); Isbel, Trutko, and Barnow (2000); and Krueger and Rouse (1998).	Limited evidence based on national employer data, selected JTPA-supported training programs, and data for specific firms.	Contract training enhances workers' productivity, but utilization of training differs dramatically by size and industry mix of employers.
Investigate whether, for local labor markets, the occupational skills supplied by CCs match employers' demand for skills.	Jacobson, et al. (2005) and present study.	Use data on field of study collected for individual colleges and indicators of demand for local labor markets.	Evidence for Florida suggests a correspondence between college curriculums and community and employer characteristics. Our evidence for California appears in Chapter 7.

at the local labor market level, the performance of community colleges in supplying occupational training that matches employers' demand for skills. This approach is summarized in the fourth entry of Table 4.1.

EFFECTS ON LABOR MARKET OUTCOMES

Kane and Rouse (1999) provide a survey of the limited literature, relative to that available for four-year colleges, that supplies estimates of the labor market payoffs to community college programs. Two of these studies, Kane and Rouse (1995) and Leigh and Gill (1997), were introduced in Chapter 3. Using national data, these articles demonstrate that a year's worth of credits earned at a community college is associated with a 5–8 percent increase in annual earnings, about the same impact as a year's worth of credits at a four-year college. Evidence is also presented indicating that there is a premium as high as 27 percent for earning an AA degree. Finally, the authors find that even the average community college student who enrolls but does not complete a degree or certificate still earns 6–12 percent more than the average high school graduate. In a more recent study, Gill and Leigh (2003) add evidence that the earnings of four-year college graduates who started at a community college are not substantially different from the earnings of BA degree recipients who started at a four-year college.

This literature suggests that, *on average*, enrolling in a community college does enhance earnings prospects. Nevertheless, positive average earnings effects may disguise quite different effects estimated for different programs. Grubb (1996, Chapter 3) makes the point that because occupational skills programs tend to be job-specific, the economic returns may be low or even zero if an individual cannot find training-related employment in the local labor market. Using national data from the National Longitudinal Survey of Youth (NLSY), Leigh and Gill (2001) estimate the returns to seven different fields of study. We find that the size of the earnings premium varies substantially by field of study, with engineering/computer science and social science/public service the highest-paying fields for men, and nursing the highest-paying field for women.

While some nationally representative data sets like the NLSY include information on community college field of study, more detailed and credible results require access to information for larger numbers of community college students and for geographic areas more closely aligned to local labor markets. As indicated by Grubb and others such as Mueser, Troske, and Gorislavsky (2003), the most promising approach to obtaining the desired data is to make use of administrative data available at the state level matching community college student records, which contain field of study, to individuals' earnings records obtained from Unemployment Insurance (UI) earnings histories. Grubb summarizes the results of a study of two California community colleges (Santa Barbara City College and Grossmont College) that uses data matching student records with UI wage histories. Cross tabulations presented show substantial differences in economic returns by field of study and by receipt of a degree or certificate. In a similar study that is part of the DoED Community College Labor Market Responsiveness Initiative, Jacobson et al. (2005) use student records matched with UI wage records for the Florida community college system. The authors' cross-tabulation results reveal that while there are not substantial differences in earnings prior to entering college, postcollege differences by field of study are quite large, with students who completed programs in engineering and technology earning over 45 percent more than graduates in nonvocational or leisure programs.

A larger-scale and more definitive study using student records matched with UI wage records is Jacobson, LaLonde, and Sullivan's (2005a,b) examination of the labor market payoffs to programs offered at all 25 campuses in the Washington state community college system. Their data set contains observations for over 65,000 dislocated workers who lost their jobs during the first half of the 1990s. For each dislocated worker, 14 years of quarterly earnings records are available for analysis. Making use of the longitudinal nature of the data, Jacobson, LaLonde, and Sullivan reach four main conclusions. First, they find that estimated returns to a year of community college credits are substantial—about 7–9 percent for men over age 35 and 10–13 percent for women over age 35. Second, these earnings gains are comparable in size to those for dislocated workers younger than age 35. Third, since workers' earnings may be temporarily depressed in the period immediately after leaving college, they demonstrate that it is important to have sufficient postcollege information so that long-term earnings gains can be estimated.

The final and possibly most important conclusion for this chapter is the authors' finding that earnings estimates differ substantially by major field of study. For men, large long-term quarterly earnings gains on the order of about 14 percent are obtained for academic courses in science and mathematics as well as for more technically oriented occupational skills courses, including courses in health occupations. The gains are larger for women—about 29 percent. For all other community college courses, long-term earnings gains for both males and females are close to zero.

Other than Jacobson, LaLonde, and Sullivan (2005a,b), few studies are available that use matched administrative data sets to estimate returns to alternative community college fields of study. There is clearly a need for studies that examine matched data for states other than Washington and for individuals in addition to dislocated workers. Unfortunately, researchers' access to matched state administrative records appears to have been significantly curtailed as of spring 2003 by a restrictive interpretation for the DoED of the federal Family Educational Rights Privacy Act.[1] Jacobson et al. (2005) also comment that they found it extraordinarily time consuming and difficult to obtain individual-level data on field of study linked to wage record files.

THE DoED COMMUNITY COLLEGE LABOR MARKET RESPONSIVENESS INITIATIVE

More evidence on the linkage between community college training programs and employer needs has recently been supplied by the large-scale DoED Community College Labor Market Responsiveness Initiative. This initiative produced the following major research outputs:

- A literature review intended to identify the characteristics of market-responsive community colleges.
- A three-volume handbook designed to assist community colleges to become more market driven.

- A set of three research appendices that provide additional information on the colleges and local labor markets analyzed in the initiative and a discussion of the different approaches that might be taken to measure labor market responsiveness.

We discuss each of these research outputs in turn.

Characteristics of a Labor Market-Responsive Community College

Harmon and MacAllum (2003) review over 200 articles with two questions in mind: First, is there a consensus as to what constitutes a market-responsive community college? Second, are there particular community colleges that offer exemplary market-responsive programs? In connection with the first question, their reading of the literature indicates that market-responsive colleges share several key characteristics. These include a leadership committed to a market-responsive mission, an internal response mechanism dedicated to rapidly developing new occupational skills curriculums, and close ties to local businesses and workforce and educational organizations.

Assisting Community Colleges to Become More Market Driven

Building on this literature review, the DoED initiative's second major research product is a three-volume handbook designed to assist community colleges that wish to become more market driven (MacAllum and Yoder 2004). The handbook is developed from information gained from site visits to more than 30 community colleges serving 10 distinct labor market areas scattered across the nation. Four California community colleges, all serving the San Diego metropolitan area, were visited.

Volume 1 of the handbook, titled "Unleashing the Power of the Community College," draws on interviews with college administrators and faculty as well as local employers, community-based organizations, and economic development agencies to develop seven "modules" summarizing important lessons learned from the site visits. The first three of these modules relate to a college's leadership and governance, organizational structure, and culture. More relevant to our study are the final four modules, which include the following:

1) Resources and funding. Responsive colleges look beyond traditional state funding to access a wide variety of resources including grants, local and state initiatives, federal funds, in-kind donations, and employer partnerships.

2) Information and data. Awareness of local and regional economic and workforce trends and personal contact with employers and the economic development community are crucial to responsive colleges for gathering current local labor market information.

3) Relationship-building. Responsive colleges reach out to a variety of constituents including employers and economic development agencies, industry associations, community-based organizations, K-12 systems, four-year colleges, Workforce Investment Boards, and unions.

4) Partnerships. Responsive colleges seek out partnership opportunities with employers and industry associations. Large employers and innovative industries are particularly attractive partners.

Volume 2 of the handbook, titled "Promising Practices and Lessons from the Field," provides examples from the 30 colleges visited of successful applications of these modules. In Volume 3 ("Self-Assessment Tools and Resources"), two instruments are presented that are designed to provide practical guidance to administrators for improving their colleges' labor market responsiveness. Building on the seven modules outlined in Volume 1, the first instrument is intended to help administrators identify areas that may be hindering responsiveness and develop strategies for dealing with these problem areas. The second provides administrators with a tool for assessing the needs of the local labor market.

Research Appendices

For our purposes, the DoED initiative's third major research product consisting of three research appendices is probably the most useful (Jacobson et al. 2005). In the first appendix, the authors use Integrated Postsecondary Education Data System information on key characteristics of the nation's 1,190 community colleges as well as the 30 colleges specifically examined in the handbook. Examples of these key characteristics are college enrollment and sources of institutional funding. Using cross-tabulations, the key characteristics are linked to local labor market characteristics such as city size, selected demographic statistics, and the industrial mix of the local economy. Based on this analysis, the authors conclude that colleges that offer extensive market-responsive programs tend to have

- Large enrollments.

- Substantial revenues from local government sources. As suggested by the "resources and funding" module, these revenues represent a "buy-in" from local civic and business leaders.

- A suburban location in a major metropolitan area. Consistent with the "partnerships" module, proximity to high-tech employers is especially important.

In a second appendix, Jacobson et al. (2005) describe the industrial mix of nine major labor market areas included in the study and identify differences in employer demand for alternative types of training across these nine areas. The authors find that demand-side differences between local labor markets are broadly consistent with information provided by college officials about the major skill areas in which they are developing programs and partnering with local employers.

In the final appendix, Jacobson et al. (2005) discuss the types of analyses that could be done to measure labor market responsiveness. As part of this discussion, the authors make use of student records matched with UI wage records for Florida to examine the labor market payoffs to different fields of study. As described earlier, the authors report that average labor market gains to community college training programs vary considerably. In addition, they use data for three particular Florida community colleges to look for differences in enrollment across fields of study. Their analysis is only briefly described in the appendix. However, the results indicate that there are substantial differences between colleges in curriculum emphases, and that these differences are qualitatively consistent with differences in community characteristics and the industrial mix of local employers.

CONTRACT TRAINING PROGRAMS

Contract training programs differ from regular community college curriculums in three respects. First, courses are tailored or customized to meet the training requirements of particular employers. Second, the cost of training is paid for directly by the employer or by a government entity on behalf of the employer. Contract training thus may supply an important incremental source of revenue for financially hard-pressed community colleges. Third, contract training courses are typically designed to improve the skills of incumbent workers or those of unemployed workers seeking employment with the particular employer.

Virtually all community colleges provide contract training to local employers. Dougherty (2003) points out, however, that the level of contract training activity varies across colleges. In particular, contract training varies with the size and industry mix of local employers. Using national employer data and measuring establishment size by number of employees, Dougherty reports that utilization of community colleges for formal training ranges from 26.5 percent for establishments with less than 100 employees to 57.0 percent for establishments with 500 or more employees. This positive relationship is expected for a number of reasons. Specifically, large firms as compared to small firms

- are more likely to provide formal as opposed to informal training opportunities,
- are more likely to offer a progression of jobs that aids in employee retention,
- can spread the fixed costs of training programs over a greater number of trainees,
- are more aware of community college training programs and better able to leverage government subsidies, and
- are more attractive partners to community colleges because of larger potential enrollment and greater opportunities for future economic and political payoffs.

With respect to industry mix, Dougherty (2003) reports rates of community college utilization as low as 24.1 percent and 9.4 percent, respectively, for employers in wholesale trade and retail trade. At the other extreme, community college utilization rates for employers in durable goods manufacturing and finance, insurance, and real estate are 47.1 percent and 47.0 percent, respectively. Dougherty points out that while establishment size and industry composition are related, the large differences in community college utilization he observes also arise because state subsidies for workforce training tend to favor certain industries, such as manufacturing, over others.

Turning from the incidence of contract training to its effectiveness, Isbell, Trutko, and Barnow (2000) summarize the results of a U.S. Department of Labor–funded assessment of nine exemplary contract training programs supported under the Job Training Partnership Act (JTPA). Industry affiliations of the nine employers involved in these programs include manufacturing, health care, banking, retail sales, temporary services, utilities, and transportation. Training services, which include classroom and on-the-job training as well as adult basic skills, were designed to prepare workers for specific job openings at the company sponsoring the training. Providers of training included community and technical colleges, for-profit career colleges, nonprofit community-based organizations, and employers themselves. Participants were individuals eligible for JTPA assistance who were screened according to company employment criteria.

Isbell, Trutko, and Barnow (2000) indicate that contract training yields a number of benefits. These include

- a high rate of program completion,
- placement in jobs for almost all training completers,
- hourly wages that exceed average wages for similarly skilled workers in the local area,
- uniform receipt of fringe benefits, and
- high retention rates.

Given the range of benefits of contract training, the authors raise the question of why contract training is not more widely used. They suggest that there are four main barriers. First, local labor markets must be tight so that employers face an excess demand for workers possessing occupational skills. Second, small and midsized companies may lack the critical mass of workers and resources needed to undertake contract training programs. Third, the time and effort involved in negotiating and designing a contract training program can be considerable for both the employers and the local government agency. Finally, wariness of government red tape and the uncertainty of future government support cause employers to be reluctant to committing to contract training.

A second study of contract training effectiveness by Krueger and Rouse (1998) is noteworthy for two reasons. First, it is specific to contract training supplied by community colleges. Second, it provides a useful illustration of what can be learned from a data set linking college administrative records with employer personnel files. The government-subsidized community college training was offered to incumbent workers at two midsized companies in New Jersey, and the content of training was largely adult basic education targeted to low-skilled workers. Krueger and Rouse find modest employment effects for training participants, even though there may have been negative selection into both programs. For the service company studied, there is no significant effect of the program on wage changes of participants relative to nonparticipants. However, participants were more likely to be nominated for or to win a performance award following training. For the manufacturing company examined, average wage growth for trainees is higher than for nontrainees, and trainees are more likely to bid for new jobs and to receive promotions than comparable nontrainees.

MATCHING THE SUPPLY OF TRAINING WITH OCCUPATIONAL DEMAND PROJECTIONS

So far in this chapter we have outlined three approaches that appear in the literature assessing the impact of community colleges on labor market efficiency. However, there are difficulties with each of these approaches that cause us, as indicated by the final entry of Table 4.1, to pursue still another approach. With respect to the first approach using matched student record–UI wage history data, we noted in the first section that, unfortunately, we were unable to obtain matched data for California. The second approach involves site visits such as those reported on in the DoED's Community College Labor Market Responsiveness Initiative. While site visits provide interesting examples of labor market–responsive colleges, the evidence is primarily anecdotal and may be difficult to generalize. Our objective is to move beyond anecdotes to provide quantitative evidence for all community colleges in the California Community College System. The third approach is an intriguing option, but data limitations prevent us from using contract training as a "market signal" indicator of community colleges' labor market responsiveness. As pointed out by Jacobson et al. (2005), contract training seldom shows up on most colleges' data systems, which are geared to counting enrollment in for-credit courses to meet state and local reimbursement requirements and to satisfy federal reporting requirements.

The approach we do take builds on the preliminary analysis of Jacobson et al. (2005) assessing the quality of matches between the supply and demand for training services at the local labor market level. Beginning with the supply side, we use CCCS student records that furnish data on courses completed classified by occupational Taxonomy of Programs (TOP) codes. For each CCCS college, we calculate the percentage distribution of new skills supplied across major occupational categories by a student cohort followed over a six-year period. (Three such occupational categories, for example, are business, information technology, and food and hospitality.) On the demand side, we estimate the demand for skills at the county level for the same major occupational TOP code categories. As described in Chapter 7, demand-side measures come from labor market–demand projections made by the Labor Market Information Division of California's Employment Development Department.

We then construct an index of responsiveness to measure how closely the distribution of new skills supplied by each community college is matched with demand-side occupational employment projections for the county in which the college is located. The final step in the analysis is an attempt to explain differences in the quality of matches across colleges by determinants such as those outlined by Jacobson et al. (2005). Recall from the second section that these variables include college enrollment, share of revenue from local government sources, and a suburban location in a major metropolitan area.

Note

1. We had initially planned to estimate the returns to alternative fields of study using matched data for California community college students. In California, UI wage histories are maintained by the Labor Market Information Division (LMID) of the state's Employment Development Department (EDD). We negotiated with EDD for well over a year to obtain a match between the California Community College System student records we already possessed and EDD's wage records. These negotiations eventually proved fruitless, and we turned to an alternative approach to evaluating community college responsiveness. This is the fourth approach outlined in Table 4.1.

5

Responsiveness to the Educational Needs of Immigrants by Broad Categories of Race or Ethnicity

This chapter addresses the first research question posed in Chapter 1. The question is whether California community colleges are meeting the educational needs of current and recent generations of immigrants. By educational needs, Chapter 1 specified that what we have in mind is a successful outcome of a student's community college experience. Among the major immigrant groups into the United States—Latinos and Asians—we also identified as an important national problem the low level of educational attainment of Latinos. At the same time, Asians typically possess a much higher level of educational attainment. The literature review in Chapter 3 described that common measures of educational attainment for community college students include transferring to a four-year college, receipt of an AA degree, and total number of credits earned.

The primary data source for our empirical analysis is administrative data reported by individual community colleges to the Chancellor's Office. These data are specific to the universe of first-time-freshmen (FTF) students enrolled at any CCCS campus during the 1996–1997 academic year. Members of this student cohort are followed for six years through 2002. In Appendix A, we describe the construction of our data extract from the four data files available for the 1996 FTF cohort. As explained in this appendix, after merging the four student files and appending several institutional-level variables, there are 335,615 FTF in our extract.

This chapter is organized into three main sections, the first of which describes the FTF data set and the variables we construct from these data. A primary purpose of this section is to look for differences in student characteristics and the characteristics of colleges attended that may be helpful in understanding gaps in educational attainment between major race or ethnic groups. The next section follows with an attempt to explain the gaps we observe between Latinos and whites and between Asians and whites. We seek to identify major barriers to higher educational attainment for Latinos, as well as to quantify those factors that result in Asians outperforming whites, despite disadvantages associated with recent immigration. In the third section, we break out for separate analysis two subgroups of students of particular concern to policymakers: 1) first-generation immigrants, and 2) high school dropouts. Focusing on transfer rates, we also consider the impact of individual college fixed effects to better control for differences between the individual colleges attended by community college students. The last section summarizes the main empirical results presented in the chapter.

FIRST-TIME-FRESHMEN DATA AND DESCRIPTIVE STATISTICS

Chapter 3 identified five categories of student-level variables that should be measured and included in our empirical analysis. The first of these is community college outcome variables. As just noted, these include transfer to a four-year college, receipt of an AA degree, and total credits earned. On the other side of the equation, our four categories of explanatory variables measured for individual students include 1) student preparation and background, 2) financial need, 3) students' academic goals, and 4) students' academic abilities. In addition, a fifth category of explanatory variables is measured at the institutional level. This section focuses on the measurement of these outcome and explanatory variables. We begin by addressing the critical question of how race or ethnicity is recorded in FTF data.

Measures of Race or Ethnicity

First-time-freshmen data measure race or ethnicity at two levels of detail. At the broad or "one-digit" level, categories of race or ethnicity reported are white, black, Latino, Asian, Filipino, American Indian, Pacific Islander, and other nonwhite. The distribution of FTF students at the one-digit level of race or ethnicity is shown in Table 5.1. Percentages of students in each category are calculated for the data set

Table 5.1 Descriptive Statistics for One-Digit and Two-Digit Race or Ethnicity Variables, 1996 FTF Data, by Gender (%)

Race or ethnicity variable	Males	Females
Whites	42.8	41.9
Blacks	9.8	10.6
Latinos (all)	28.3	29.3
Mexico	15.8	16.0
Central America	2.7	2.6
South America	0.9	0.9
Other Latino	2.2	2.2
Undesignated Latino	6.7	7.6
Asians (all)	11.3	11.2
China	2.9	3.2
India	0.5	0.5
Japan	0.8	0.9
Korea	1.0	1.1
Laos	0.2	0.2
Cambodia	0.2	0.3
Vietnam	2.5	2.1
Other Asian	1.1	0.9
Undesignated Asian	2.1	2.0
Filipino	3.4	3.0
American Indian	1.5	1.4
Pacific Islander	0.8	0.7
Other nonwhite	2.0	1.9
Number of students	148,508	156,751

we obtain after imposing three restrictions on observations included in our data extract:

1) respondents must be reported as male or female (i.e., we omit the "other" gender category),

2) respondents' ages must be between 17 and 60, and

3) respondents' race or ethnicity must be reported (i.e., we omit the "unknown" and "declined to state" categories).

Application of the first restriction removes only a handful of community college students from the data set. The second and third restrictions are more important and are roughly equally binding. Their combined impact is to reduce the number of individuals included in our data set from 335,615 students to 305,259 students. We stratify by gender in the table based on a paper by Surette (2001) that shows, using national data, that female students are much less likely to transfer than males. Slightly over 51 percent of students in our data set are female.

Collection and reporting of data at the one-digit level are required by the Chancellor's Office. The Chancellor's Office also instructs individual colleges to report, if collected, additional detail on Latino and Asian students' country or region of family origin. These "two-digit" ethnicity categories are listed in Table 5.1. In addition to the detailed ethnicity, the table distinguishes an "other" category from an "undesignated" category. The "other" category is reported in FTF data, and it indicates for Latinos, for example, a student whose two-digit designation is a heritage other than Mexican, Central American, or South American. In contrast, "undesignated" is a category we define to capture individuals who report a one-digit category of Latino but no two-digit category of Mexico, Central America, South America, or other Latino. Given the large percentage of students of Mexican ancestry, it is quite likely that the bulk of undesignated Latinos belong in the Mexican category. However, we have no way of knowing which ones are really Mexican Americans. Two-digit ethnicity categories, including the undesignated category, sum up to one-digit totals.

At the one-digit level, Table 5.1 shows that the largest racial or ethnic category of students is whites at about 42 percent. Latinos follow at about 29 percent, then Asians (including Filipinos) at about 14 percent, and finally blacks at about 10 percent. Gender differences in the race/ethnicity distributions at the one-digit level are minor.

The more detailed two-digit breakdowns of Latino and Asian students shown in Table 5.1 correspond closely to the immigration statistics presented in Chapter 1 for California and the entire United States. That is, most Latino community college students are of Mexican ancestry, and Latino immigrants to California are primarily from Mexico. Similarly, the table shows that the largest categories of Asian students are Chinese, Filipino, and Vietnamese, followed at a distance by Indians, Koreans, and Japanese. Table 1.1 in Chapter 1 (p. 9) indicated that the Philippines, China, India, and Vietnam, in that order, send the greatest numbers of Asian immigrants to California.

The empirical analysis presented in this chapter is based on the one-digit breakdown of race or ethnicity. In Chapter 6, we exploit the greater race/ethnicity detail available for Latino and Asian students.

Community College Outcome Variables

The three community college outcome variables displayed in Table 5.2 capture alternative measures of success in a student's community college experience. Transfer to a four-year college represents the successful accomplishment of an important step in the academic program of students who aspire to a BA degree. From a policy point of view, failure to transfer to a four-year college in sufficient numbers is a key factor in understanding why Latinos lag behind whites in overall educational attainment. Receipt of an AA or AS degree signals the completion of an academic program that serves as a stepping stone for further course work at a four-year institution. But an AA degree may also represent completion of a two-year occupational training program. In connection with total credits earned, Kane and Rouse (1995) draw attention to the

Table 5.2 Descriptive Statistics for Community College Outcome Variables, by One-Digit Race or Ethnicity Categories and Gender

Outcome variable	Latinos	Whites	Blacks	Asians[a]
		Males		
Transfer (%)	7.4	14.9	9.5	25.4
Receipt of AA or AS degree (%)	5.7	8.1	5.2	10.7
Semester-equivalent credits earned	21.8	24.9	17.3	35.6
Number of students	42,070	63,551	14,482	21,957
		Females		
Transfer (%)	9.0	16.3	8.9	27.7
Receipt of AA or AS degree (%)	9.6	11.8	6.6	15.8
Semester-equivalent credits earned	27.2	28.1	20.0	38.0
Number of students	45,962	65,668	16,563	22,231

[a]Includes Filipinos.

fact that many community college students complete very few credits. We view total credits earned as capturing the persistence needed to successfully complete either a traditional transfer-oriented program or a stand-alone occupational training program. Total credits earned are expressed in terms of semester equivalents, and all three outcome variables are measured over the six-year window between 1996 and 2002.[1]

In addition to distinguishing males and females as in Table 5.1, we further disaggregate in Table 5.2 by broad categories of race or ethnicity. Beginning with student transfers, Appendix A notes that FTF data track community college student transfers to any four-year college, whether public or private or California or out of state. Our impression from the data is that the vast majority of student transfers are in-state and to a UC or CSU campus. Among males, the transfer rate calculated for white students is exactly double that for Latinos (14.9 percent versus 7.4 percent). At the same time, the transfer rate for Asian students is nearly double that of whites (or nearly four times that of Latinos). African Americans transfer at a rate that is above that of Latinos but well below the rate of whites. In the lower half of the table, transfer rates are slightly higher for females than males within all race/ethnicity categories, except for blacks. Not shown in Table 5.2, overall female and male transfer rates are 14.9 percent and 13.7 percent, respectively. Differences for females across race/ethnicity categories are very similar to those just discussed for males. That is, the transfer rate for Asians is much higher than that for whites (27.7 percent versus 16.3 percent), and the white rate exceeds that for Latinos and blacks.

Before moving to the other outcome variables, two further points should be made in connection with transfer rates. First, the rates appear low in comparison to the national transfer rate of 25 percent measured as of 1989–1990 (Bradburn and Hurst 2001). One difference is that the national rate is calculated excluding first-time community college students taking only noncredit courses. As indicated in Appendix A, however, imposing this restriction reduces the number of California students by only 608 individuals, which makes no difference in calculating the transfer rate. A more important consideration is the difference in students' academic goals. At the national level, Bradburn and Hurst indicate that 71 percent of entering community college students anticipate earning a bachelor's degree or higher. Looking ahead to Table 5.3, the Educational Goals section of the table indicates that only about 35 percent of entering California students plan to transfer to a four-year institution. Instead, large fractions of students express an interest in enhancing their occupational skills or in pursuing a basic skills curriculum. Others are "undecided" at the time they first enrolled. As suggested by the discussion in Chapter 2, a broad diversity in student academic goals reflects the ready access to California's community colleges made possible by an open-admission policy, low tuition, and conveniently located campuses.

The second point is that there are a number of alternative ways to calculate transfer rates. One possibility using FTF data is to calculate three-year as well as six-year transfer rates. Wassmer, Moore, and Shulock (2004) follow up on this possibility and report that the three-year rate is much lower than the six-year rate. This result is expected in view of the large number of community college students attending school on a part-time basis. It is also common to calculate transfer rates only for community college students who somehow indicate an intention to transfer. To isolate on the population of "transfer-eligible" students, Wassmer, Moore, and Shulock examine only those students who completed at least 12 credits and enrolled in transfer-level math or English courses. As they note, however, there is considerable debate in the literature over the criteria to impose in deciding exactly which students to exclude. Our approach is to take the most inclusive approach possible using FTF data. This means that we measure transfers in a six-year rather than three-year window, and retain for analysis all students included in our data set. By including all students in the data set, we allow for the possibility that exposure to a community college may positively affect educational aspirations, making every student a potential transfer student.

An AA degree is seen in Table 5.2 to be a much less common outcome than is transferring to a four-year college. The single exception to this statement occurs for female Latinos, for whom the AA receipt rate is 9.6 percent as opposed to a transfer rate of 9.0 percent. Otherwise, results for AA receipt generally echo those for transfers. For both males and females, that is, AA receipt is higher for whites than Latinos and blacks, and higher for Asians than whites. Associate's degree receipt is about the same for Latinos and black males, but higher for Latino females than black females. Asian female students display the highest percentage of AA degree recipients at 15.8 percent, while the lowest

Table 5.3 Descriptive Statistics for Student-Level Explanatory Variables, Males Only, by One-Digit Race/Ethnicity Categories

Variable name	Latinos	Whites	Blacks	Asians[a]
Background variables				
High school or other degree				
U.S. high school diploma	0.654	0.751	0.704	0.621
Foreign high school diploma	0.064	0.024	0.023	0.201
GED	0.063	0.070	0.087	0.032
Other degree	0.067	0.087	0.065	0.064
No high school diploma	0.152	0.068	0.121	0.083
Took or needs ESL	0.104	0.014	0.016	0.203
Basic skills courses/all courses	0.174	0.060	0.112	0.127
Citizenship status				
U.S. citizen	0.694	0.915	0.931	0.467
Permanent resident	0.247	0.034	0.031	0.388
Other	0.059	0.051	0.038	0.145
Financial need				
Age at first term				
17–25	0.714	0.683	0.675	0.770
26–60	0.285	0.316	0.325	0.229
Semester-equivalent credits attempted/semester	6.89	7.30	7.46	8.32
Educational goals				
Transferring with or without AA	0.298	0.358	0.385	0.438
AA without plans to transfer	0.051	0.046	0.059	0.046
Enhancing occupational skills	0.309	0.264	0.268	0.171
Educational development	0.109	0.082	0.091	0.103
Undecided	0.208	0.222	0.175	0.218
Uncollected or unreported	0.026	0.028	0.022	0.024
Community college progress variables				
GPA[b]	1.98	2.34	1.84	2.25
Credits earned/credits attempted[c]	0.516	0.601	0.437	0.595
Courses transferable to UCs and CSUs/all courses taken	0.357	0.434	0.428	0.477
Number of students	42,070	63,551	14,482	21,957
Percent of total students	29.6	44.7	10.2	15.5

[a] Includes Filipinos.
[b] Omits students who took only nongraded courses.
[c] Omits students who took no classes for credit.

percentage is for black males at 5.2 percent. Overall, the percentage of females receiving an AA degree over the period of observation exceeds that of males 11.1 percent to 7.4 percent.

The total credits earned variable appearing in Table 5.2 is measured in semester-equivalent terms to take account of the fact that a small number of CCCS colleges operate on quarter systems rather than semesters. We multiplied quarter credits by two-thirds and added them to semester credits to arrive at "semester-equivalent" credits. The average student at a CCCS college completed over his or her community college career between 24 and 28 credits, or between 0.82 and 0.94 of the credits that would be earned in one year of full-time college attendance (30 semester credits).

The table indicates a large gap in total semester-equivalent credits earned between Asian students and all others. Among female students, Asians average 38 total credits earned over their community college careers. This compares to 28.1 credits earned for whites, 27.2 credits for Latinos, and 20.0 credits for blacks. Among males, Asians average 35.6 credits as compared to 24.9 credits for whites, the next highest race/ethnicity category.

Background Variables

Turning to student-level explanatory variables, we measure students' academic background and preparation using FTF information on high school degree, citizenship, and need for remedial courses at the community college level. Still disaggregating by one-digit race or ethnicity, Table 5.3 shows for males that whites are most likely to have earned a U.S. high school diploma, followed by blacks, then Latinos, and finally Asians. Just 62.1 percent of Asian male students possess a U.S. high school diploma. However, 20 percent of Asian males hold a foreign high school degree. Lumping together U.S. and foreign high school degrees, Asians are even more likely than whites to have earned a high school diploma (82.2 percent versus 77.5 percent). At 71.8 percent, Latino males are least likely to hold a high school degree. Over 15 percent of Latino male students are high school dropouts.

Consistent with the result that many Asians received their K-12 education outside the United States is the finding that 20.3 percent of Asian male students have taken or are in need of community college

ESL courses. This compares to about 10 percent of Latinos and only 1.4 percent of whites needing ESL. Nevertheless, it is interesting to note that the ratio of community college basic skills courses (courses that include remedial reading and math as well as ESL) to all courses is lower for Asians (12.7 percent) than for Latinos (17.4 percent).

First-time-freshmen data measure citizenship rather than country of birth. However, it seems very likely that the vast majority of the 92–93 percent of white and black male students who are U.S. citizens are also native-born Americans. Only about 3 percent of both whites and blacks are permanent residents, who are first-generation immigrants holding "green cards" that allow them residence in the United States. In contrast, Latino and especially Asian students are much more likely to be first-generation immigrants. Table 5.3 shows that nearly 25 percent of Latino males and 39 percent of Asian males are immigrants with permanent residency status. Another 5.9 percent of Latinos and 14.5 percent of Asians fall into the "other" citizenship status category, which includes "temporary" residents holding H1-B visas, individuals holding student F1 or M1 visas, refugees or asylees, and individuals with some other or an unknown status. We delve into the details of the other citizenship category in Chapter 6, when we focus on the two-digit level of ethnicity available for Latinos and Asians. At this point, however, it is worth emphasizing that at least 53 percent of Asian male students in our data set are first-generation immigrants. We apply the phrase "at least" because it is likely that other Asian students are first-generation immigrants who have made it through the citizenship process. At least 31 percent of Latino male students in our data set are first-generation immigrants.

Differences between male and female students on the background variables tend to be slight, and we note just a few. For female students described in Table 5.4, the main differences from males are that, except for Asians, females are somewhat more likely to be U.S. citizens and to have earned a U.S. high school degree. Among Asian students, females are slightly less likely than males to be U.S. citizens and graduates of American high schools.

Table 5.4 Descriptive Statistics for Student-Level Explanatory Variables, Females Only, by One-Digit Race/Ethnicity Categories

Variable name	Latinos	Whites	Blacks	Asians[a]
Background variables				
High school or other degree				
U.S. high school diploma	0.686	0.770	0.718	0.587
Foreign high school diploma	0.064	0.040	0.021	0.243
GED	0.055	0.063	0.074	0.023
Other degree	0.056	0.055	0.054	0.070
No high school diploma	0.139	0.073	0.133	0.077
Took or needs ESL	0.117	0.021	0.013	0.252
Basic skills courses/all courses	0.199	0.075	0.139	0.152
Citizenship status				
U.S. citizen	0.713	0.930	0.948	0.442
Permanent resident	0.246	0.048	0.026	0.412
Other	0.040	0.023	0.025	0.146
Financial need				
Age at first term				
17–25	0.703	0.642	0.631	0.711
26–60	0.297	0.357	0.370	0.290
Semester-equivalent credits attempted/semester	7.18	7.31	7.60	8.04
Educational goals				
Transferring with or without AA	0.311	0.343	0.338	0.407
AA without plans to transfer	0.054	0.052	0.059	0.056
Enhancing occupational skills	0.281	0.266	0.316	0.169
Educational development	0.118	0.093	0.098	0.129
Undecided	0.210	0.217	0.169	0.211
Uncollected or unreported	0.025	0.029	0.029	0.027
Community college progress variables				
GPA[b]	2.09	2.48	1.85	2.55
Credits earned/credits attempted[c]	0.550	0.617	0.437	0.663
Courses transferable to UCs and CSUs/all courses taken	0.390	0.471	0.409	0.465
Number of students	45,962	65,668	16,563	22,231
Percent of total students	30.6	43.6	11.0	14.8

[a] Includes Filipinos.

[b] Omits students who took only nongraded courses.

[c] Omits students who took no classes for credit.

Financial Need

First-time-freshmen data do not provide information on family background. Hence, we do not have a direct measure of a student's financial capacity to attend college without having to work at least part time. We do, however, develop two proxy variables to capture financial need. The first is whether the student is older than age 25. An age of 25 is commonly used in the literature to distinguish students who entered college immediately after completing high school from students who worked for a period of time after high school and then entered college. Four examples of articles that make use of this age threshold are Alfonso (2006); Chancellor's Office (2002); Wassmer, Moore, and Shulock (2004); and Alfonso, Bailey, and Scott (2005). The first three of these papers were summarized in Chapter 3. Alfonso, Bailey, and Scott (2005) provide empirical support for the over-25 age variable reporting that their nonlinearity test of the effect of age indicates that students aged 26 and older are different from younger students.

The literature indicates that the transfer rate of students 25 years of age and younger considerably exceeds that of older students. Three considerations underlie this result. The first is that younger students may still be able to draw on the resources of their parents while attending school. In contrast, students entering college beyond age 25 are more likely to be financially independent of their parents. As noted by Alfonso, Bailey, and Scott (2005), students who can rely on their parents' income are more likely to be able to attend college in a more "traditional" fashion. A second consideration is that age exceeding 25 indicates students who delay college entry after high school, a factor generally associated with a reduced probability of graduation. Finally, as noted by Sengupta and Jepsen (2006), older students are more likely than younger students to focus on occupational skills courses that will put them in a better position for raises and promotions with their current employers.

Overall, approximately 30 percent of male students and 33 percent of female students in the FTF data set entered community college at an age older than 25. For both male and female students, Tables 5.3 and 5.4 show that Asians tend to be younger than students in the other race/ethnicity categories. While older than Asians, Latino students are younger on average than whites and blacks.

Our second financial need variable seeks to measure the need to combine college attendance with employment. Alfonso, Bailey, and Scott (2005) summarize evidence relating to four-year colleges showing that full-time attendance promotes degree completion, while delaying and interrupting enrollment and working off-campus negatively affect completion. These authors and Alfonso (2006) use monthly enrollment information available in the Beginning Postsecondary Student Longitudinal Study to construct a measure of cumulative full-time equivalent (FTE) semesters in which a student is enrolled during a five-year window. Number of FTE semesters is shown to be strongly related to educational attainment.

Rather than focusing on full-time enrollment, we use FTF data on credits attempted and semesters enrolled to construct an indicator of part-time enrollment. This measure divides total credits attempted over the six years a student is observed by total semesters in which he or she is enrolled. After adjusting for the small number of credits taken at quarter-based colleges, the typical student, both male and female, attempted slightly less than 7.5 semester credits per semester in the semesters in which he or she was enrolled. That is, students typically maintained a half-time course load during their community college careers. Across race/ethnicity categories, Tables 5.3 and 5.4 indicate that male and female Asians carry a considerably higher course load than whites or blacks. Typical course loads taken by whites and blacks, in turn, exceed those of Latinos.

Educational Goals

A solid academic background and basic competence in English are generally a necessary but not sufficient criterion for a successful community college experience. With respect to transferring to a four-year college, students must also have an interest in pursuing a transfer-oriented curriculum. Alternative career objectives that do not involve transferring include occupational skills training necessary for immediate employment or advancement in the student's current job. Using educational goals of FTF uninformed by counseling, we collapse into five categories the 13 possible goals identified in FTF data and listed in Appendix A. These include 1) transferring, either with or without an AA degree, 2) earning an AA degree without planning to transfer,

3) enhancing occupational skills, 4) educational development, which includes training in basic skills, and 5) undecided.

Tables 5.3 and 5.4 indicate that Asians generally are much more likely than other students to express an interest in transferring, either with or without an AA degree. For instance, Table 5.3 shows that nearly 44 percent of Asian males report an interest in transferring as opposed to about 39 percent of black males, 36 percent of white males, and 30 percent of Latino males. About 31 percent of Latino males enroll in a community college with the goal of enhancing occupational skills. Table 5.4 shows that only black females report greater interest in occupational skills training. Overall, female students, except for Latinos, exhibit slightly less interest in transferring than males. Among Latinos, females show somewhat more interest than males in transferring and a slightly lower interest in occupational skills.

Community College Progress Variables

We measure students' academic abilities indirectly by their performance while enrolled in a community college. These measures include

- grade point average (GPA) calculated over courses taken for credit and for a letter grade,
- ratio of credits earned to credits attempted calculated for students who took classes for credit, and
- ratio of courses transferable to both UC and CSU campuses to all courses taken.[2]

What we are trying to accomplish with these variables is to describe students who have the ability and interest to complete transferable courses in a timely manner with letter grades that meet admissions thresholds established by state four-year universities.

Table 5.3 shows that Asian and white male students are roughly comparable on these academic progress variables. For instance, white males have a slightly higher GPA than Asian males (2.34 vs. 2.25), while Asian males have a slightly higher transferable course ratio than whites (0.477 vs. 0.434). Latino and black males lag behind whites and Asians on all three progress measures. Especially striking are the low ratio of credits completed for blacks (0.437) and the low transferable course ratio for Latinos (0.357). Table 5.4 indicates that, except for blacks, female students tend to perform slightly better than males. Means for all three progress variables are virtually identical for male and female black students.

College-Level Explanatory Variables

Since FTF data provide information on the community college each student attended, we can add to our student records variables measured at the college level that are likely to affect a student's chances of transferring. Recall from the literature review in Chapter 3 that Ehrenberg and Smith (2004) and Wassmer, Moore, and Shulock (2004) recommend use of individual-level data linked to college-level data.

The diversion effect literature summarized in Chapter 3 emphasizes the importance of a community college's academic "culture" in determining whether an entering student aspiring to a BA degree will make progress towards this goal by successfully transferring, or will be diverted from his or her goal. As shown in Table 5.5, our measures of a college's culture include

- freshman students' performance on standardized tests measured by the Academic Preparation Index (API),
- emphasis on transfer programs as measured by the ratio of transfer credits to all credits,
- proximity to a four-year college as measured by distance to nearest UC and nearest CSU campuses, and
- median household income in the community in which the college is located and the percentage of community residents with a BA degree or higher.

The API measures the mean for every CCCS community college of its entering freshmen's scores on standardized exams students took as high school juniors during the 1997–1998 and 1998–1999 academic years. This index is reported in Office of Planning, Research, and Grants Development (2002). Since we append the college-level variables to FTF student records, mean values of API reported in Table 5.5 are calculated over all student observations rather than over CCCS colleges. Hence, the means we report are really weighted averages of all the college means, where the weight applied to each college's individual mean is the proportion of all FTF in the system that enrolled in the particular

Table 5.5 Descriptive Statistics for College-Level Explanatory Variables, Males Only, by One-Digit Race/Ethnicity Categories

Variable name	Latinos	Whites	Blacks	Asians[a]
Academic Preparation Index	45.9	49.1	45.9	48.0
Transfer credits/all credits (%)	73.6	75.5	74.2	77.0
Miles to nearest UC	34.1	42.1	28.0	25.6
Miles to nearest CSU	18.0	20.7	15.6	12.7
Median household income ($,000)	48.4	50.6	47.6	55.4
Percentage BA degree	25.7	27.7	27.7	33.4
Number of observations	42,070	63,551	14,482	21,957

[a] Includes Filipinos.

college. Minimum and maximum values reported in the table have the usual interpretation of the smallest and largest values of the API measured across all 106 campuses included in our data set.

The transfer emphasis, proximity, and community income and education variables appear in Gill and Leigh (2004). As described in Chapter 2, in that project we put together a large data set measuring for each California community college the mix of academic programs offered along with measures of community characteristics and campus-specific characteristics. Our objective was to investigate whether colleges choose different missions as captured in differences in mix of programs offered and, if they do, whether these differences can be accounted for by differences in community needs and special attributes of individual colleges.

Table 5.5 presents means, for male students, of our college-level explanatory variables stratified by race or ethnicity. (Means for female students are virtually identical.) Differences in API and the ratio of transfer credits to all credits are small. The main difference across race/ethnicity categories is for measures of proximity of the community college to a UC or CSU campus. The table indicates that Asian students attend community colleges closer in proximity to UC and CSU campuses than blacks and Latinos, with community colleges attended by whites furthest away on average from the nearest state four-year universities. This suggests that Asians tend to be more concentrated in major metropolitan areas, while whites are more evenly dispersed across the state. Consistent with this observation is the finding that colleges attended by

Asians are located in higher-income, more highly educated communities. The API and transfer credits ratio indicate that whites and Asians, in comparison to Latinos, attend colleges that enroll slightly better prepared students and are somewhat more transfer oriented.

Summary

Thus far in this chapter we have identified gaps in three community college outcome measures between Latinos and whites and between Asians and whites. Latinos lag behind whites on all three measures, especially the transfer rate. Among our student-level explanatory variables, possible candidates to explain observed Latino-whites gaps include a deficient high school background, a high proportion of recent immigrants, a greater obligation to work while attending college, less interest in ultimately transferring to a four-year college as opposed to other goals, and poorer academic performance while in college. On the other hand, Latino students tend to be somewhat younger than whites, a factor that is related to a higher transfer rate. Measured at the institutional level, in addition, we find some small differences between the community colleges attended by Latinos and whites. The colleges attended by Latinos tend to be less transfer oriented, to have student bodies that are generally less well prepared for college, and to be located in less affluent communities. At the same time, colleges attended by Latinos are typically closer to UC and CSU campuses.

The situation is quite different for Asians. Asian students exceed whites on all three community college outcome measures, with especially large gaps calculated for transfer rates and total credits earned. To explain these gaps, we reported that differences in our explanatory variables often, but not always, favor Asians over whites. Beginning with immigration status, we noted that less than half of Asian students are U.S. citizens. As a consequence of their recent immigration status, Asians are more likely than whites to express a need for ESL and to take remedial community college courses. At the same time, Asian students are both younger and slightly more likely than whites to possess a high school degree (combining both foreign and U.S. degrees). Moreover, Asians carry a higher course load and are more likely to express an interest in ultimately transferring. An open question is whether the higher proportion of foreign high school graduates really represents a disadvantage for Asian students. Asians and whites appear to perform equally well in community college classrooms. At the institutional level, differences between Asians and whites tend to be small. The main difference is that Asians attend colleges that are in closer proximity to a four-year university. Also, Asian students are somewhat more likely than whites to attend colleges located in affluent communities.

BASIC RESULTS FOR COMMUNITY COLLEGE OUTCOME VARIABLES

Tables 5.6 and 5.7 present for male and female students, respectively, regression estimates of the effects of the five categories of explanatory variables on our three educational outcomes.[3] Race or ethnicity variables are also included in these regressions, but we defer discussion of their estimated effects until later in the section when we assess in Table 5.8 our ability to explain observed race/ethnicity gaps in the outcome variables. Because students are clustered within community colleges, standard errors are corrected using a robust variance-covariance matrix to account for serial correlation within institutions.

Two additional points should be made at the outset about these estimates. First, we should be clear on their interpretation. For transfer and AA receipt, the regression parameters are linear probability estimates.[4] Thus, their interpretation is in terms of the estimated effect on the probability of transferring or of receiving an AA degree. Total credits earned is a continuous variable, and estimated parameters shown in the third column measure the effect on total credits of a one-unit change in each explanatory variable. Second, we omit from the right-hand side of the total credits earned regression the credits earned ratio. The reason is that credits earned appears as both the dependent variable and the numerator of the credits earned ratio, thus resulting in a built-in positive correlation with this explanatory variable.

Background Variables

Many of our a priori expectations regarding the effects of our background variables are not confirmed in Tables 5.6 and 5.7. Beginning

Table 5.6 OLS Estimates of the Determinants of Transfer to a Four-Year College, Receipt of AA Degree, and Total Credits Earned, Male Students

Variable[a]	Transfer	AA degree	Total credits earned[b]
Constant	−0.378**	−0.151**	−21.87**
Race or ethnicity			
Latinos	−0.021**	0.004	1.87**
Blacks	−0.007	0.000	−3.14**
Asians[c]	0.074**	0.006	4.02**
Background			
Schooling			
Foreign high school diploma	−0.003	0.013**	−0.68
GED	−0.026**	−0.008**	−4.35**
Other education	−0.013	−0.015**	−3.61**
No high school diploma	−0.016**	−0.001	−3.65**
Took or needs ESL	−0.020	0.019**	8.92**
Basic skills courses/all courses	−0.009	−0.022**	−6.45**
Citizenship status			
Permanent resident	0.009	0.000	2.77**
Other	0.014	0.019**	3.08**
Financial need			
Over age 25	−0.054**	−0.016**	−4.40**
Semester-equiv. credits attempted/ semester	0.012**	0.013**	3.13**
Educational goals			
Transferring with or without AA	0.049**	0.015**	3.24**
AA without plans to transfer	−0.035**	0.016**	0.80
Occupational skills	−0.014**	−0.007**	−1.20**
Educational development	−0.027	−0.015**	−1.42**
Uncollected	0.009	0.005	0.58
Community college progress variables			
GPA	0.034**	0.021**	8.66**
GPA missing	0.042**	0.020**	−13.49**
Credits earned/credits attempted	0.175**	0.129**	
Credits ratio missing	0.074**	0.034**	
Transferable courses/all courses	0.183**	0.064**	6.74**

(continued)

Table 5.6 (continued)

Variable[a]	Transfer	AA degree	Total credits earned[b]
College-specific			
Academic Preparation Index	0.003**	0.000	0.08
Transfer credits/all credits	0.024	−0.043	1.32
Miles to nearest UC	0.000	0.000	−0.01
Miles to nearest CSU	0.000	0.000	−0.02
Median household income	0.000	0.000	0.00
Percentage BA	0.000	0.000	0.03
R^2	0.204	0.124	0.456

NOTE: **Statistically significant at the 0.05 level. $N = 142,060$.

[a] Reference group categories for the dummy explanatory variables are as follows: white skin color, U.S. high school graduate, doesn't need ESL, U.S. citizen, 25 years of age or younger, and undecided on educational goals.

[b] Omitted from this relationship is the credits-earned ratio.

[c] Includes Filipinos.

with educational background, we anticipated, in comparison to possession of a U.S. high school diploma, that a foreign diploma, GED, "other" education, and no high school diploma would each have a negative effect on educational outcomes. Instead, we find in Tables 5.6 and 5.7 that a foreign high school degree has a negative and statistically significant effect in only one of the six regressions—the transfer probability of female students. For the remaining relationships, a foreign high school degree has essentially no effect save for the probability that a male student earns an AA degree. In this case, a foreign high school diploma actually increases by 1.3 percentage points the chance of receiving an AA degree. The other measures of educational background (GED, other education, and no high school diploma) all have the anticipated negative effects, and several of these estimates are statistically significant. In the total credits earned relationships, for example, failure to earn a high school degree (either U.S. or foreign) depresses number of credits earned by 3–4 credits.

Another unexpected result is the positive effect estimated for the took/needs ESL variable in the AA degree and total credits earned equations. This finding holds for both men and women. However, the broader basic skills course ratio has the expected negative effect for all three outcome measures, and parameter estimates are statistically significant except in the transfer relationship for men. The estimated effects, nevertheless, are not large. For an AA degree, the estimates suggest that taking 30 percent of courses in basic skills as opposed to, say, 10 percent, depresses the probability of an AA degree by 0.4 of a percentage point for males and 1.4 percentage points for females. The same 20-percentage-point increase in the basic skills ratio reduces credits earned by about half a credit for males and 1.7 credits for females.

Also unanticipated in Tables 5.6 and 5.7 is the absence of a statistically significant negative effect for our two non-U.S. citizen variables (permanent resident and "other" citizenship). Indeed, the noncitizen variables are estimated to increase total credits earned, other things equal, by 3–4 credits. Taken at face value, these estimates suggest that recent immigrants suffer very little disadvantage in terms of a successful community college experience in comparison to native-born Americans and immigrants who have become citizens.[5]

Other Student-Level Variables

In contrast to the educational background and citizenship variables, estimated impacts of our other student-level explanatory variables are consistent with expectations. Beginning with the financial needs variables, Tables 5.6 and 5.7 indicate that older students on entering college are less successful in comparison to students in the traditional college-age range of 18–25. In the transfer relationships, for example, age exceeding 25 is found to depress the probability of transferring by over 5 percentage points for men and nearly 8 percentage points for women. Ability to carry a larger course load has the anticipated positive effect on educational outcomes. For example, averaging a full-time class schedule of 15 hours per semester rather than a part-time schedule of, say, 7 hours per semester increases transfer probability by 9.6 percentage points ($= 0.012 \times 8$) for both male and female students.

Turning to educational goals, estimated effects shown in Tables 5.6 and 5.7 are also generally consistent with our a priori expectations. In particular, a transfer goal has a positive effect in the transfer relationships of about 5 percentage points for males and nearly 6 percentage points for females. The reference group in this comparison is students who are "undecided" in terms of their educational goals. While this

Table 5.7 OLS Estimates of the Determinants of Transfer to a Four-Year College, Receipt of AA Degree, and Total Credits Earned, Female Students

Variable[a]	Transfer	AA degree	Total credits earned[b]
Constant	−0.414**	−0.209**	−19.41**
Race or ethnicity			
Latinas	−0.020**	0.012**	3.02**
Blacks	−0.001	−0.002	−2.26**
Asians[c]	0.088**	0.014**	2.60**
Background			
Schooling			
Foreign high school diploma	−0.023**	−0.001	−0.56
GED	0.000	−0.011**	−3.40**
Other education	−0.011	−0.014**	−3.04**
No high school diploma	−0.030**	−0.001	−3.22**
Took or needs ESL	−0.010	0.021**	8.74**
Basic skills courses/all courses	−0.026**	−0.072**	−8.73**
Citizenship status			
Permanent resident	0.000	0.000	4.09**
Other	0.002	0.027**	4.07**
Financial need			
Over age 25	−0.078**	−0.015**	−4.24**
Semester-equiv. credits attempted/ semester	0.012**	0.019**	3.50**
Educational goals			
Transferring with or without AA	0.055**	0.024**	3.36**
AA without plans to transfer	−0.040**	0.012**	1.35**
Occupational skills	−0.021**	−0.015**	−1.53**
Educational development	0.025	−0.024**	−1.92**
Uncollected	0.006	0.005	−0.25
Community college progress variables			
GPA	0.035**	0.026**	8.98**
GPA missing	0.062**	0.049**	−14.02**
Credits earned/credits attempted	0.189**	0.190**	
Credits ratio missing	0.086**	0.062**	
Transferable courses/all courses	0.192**	0.063**	6.30**

Table 5.7 (continued)

Variable[a]	Transfer	AA degree	Total credits earned[b]
College-specific			
Academic Preparation Index	0.003**	0.000	−0.06
Transfer credits/all credits	0.065	−0.011	4.75
Miles to nearest UC	0.000	0.000	0.01
Miles to nearest CSU	0.000	0.000	−0.01
Median HH income	0.000	0.000	0.00
Percentage BA	0.000	0.000	0.04
R^2	0.218	0.161	0.513

NOTE: **Statistically significant at the .05 level. $N = 150{,}424$.

[a] Reference group categories for the dummy explanatory variables are as follows: white skin color, U.S. high school graduate, doesn't need ESL, U.S. citizen, 25 years of age or younger, and undecided on educational goals.

[b] Omitted from this relationship is the credits-earned ratio.

[c] Includes Filipinas.

result for the transfer outcome is expected, we also find that a transfer goal raises the probability of earning an AA degree and increases number of credits earned. For example, a female student who intends to transfer has a 2.4-percentage-point-higher chance of receiving an AA degree and is expected to earn 3.4 credits more than a comparable student who is undecided in terms of her educational goals. On the other hand, the goal of pursuing an occupational skills program is found to have a negative effect, for both males and females, on all three outcome variables.

Estimates obtained for the community college progress variables in Tables 5.6 and 5.7 suggest that making good grades, completing classes, and taking transferable courses have the expected positive effect on educational outcomes. For men, for example, a one letter grade higher GPA increases a student's transfer probability by 3.4 percentage points, the probability of an AA degree by 2.1 percentage points, and total credits earned by 8.7 credits. Estimates for women are very similar.

Since academic progress is itself likely to hinge on educational background, it may be the case that the progress variables are diluting the effects of educational background, leading to the small and often statistically insignificant parameter estimates discussed earlier in this section. To check this possibility, we estimated the educational outcome relationships excluding the academic progress variables. By far the biggest change among the explanatory variables is found for the basic skills course ratio. For this variable, excluding the academic progress variables has the effect of making substantially more negative estimates obtained for both men and women in all three outcome relationships. It is clear that in addition to its direct effect on final educational outcomes, taking more basic skills courses has the important indirect effect rate of slowing students' progress through their programs. A similar indirect effect, but of smaller magnitude, is found for absence of a high school degree. On the other hand, parameter estimates obtained for foreign high school diploma and our ESL variable are little affected by omitting the community college progress variables.

College-Level Explanatory Variables

Once we have controlled for the student-level explanatory variables, the six college-level variables shown in Tables 5.6 and 5.7 appear to have little impact on the educational outcomes. Only the API variable representing the academic quality of entering students has a statistically significant effect in the transfer equations, and the magnitude of this effect is small. Taken at face value, these results suggest that individual characteristics are much more strongly related to successful student outcomes than are institutional factors.

Bailey et al. (2005) reach the same conclusion in a study, like ours, in which individual student characteristics are merged with institutional variables. Student-level variables are taken from the National Educational Longitudinal Study of 1988, and four categories of institutional variables are developed from the Integrated Postsecondary Education Data System (IPEDS). Institutional measures include 1) general institutional characteristics such as college size, proportion of faculty working part time, and mix of certificates and AA degrees; 2) measures of student body composition; 3) financial variables such as tuition, federal student aid per FTE, and average expenditures per FTE on instruction, academic support, student services, and administration; and 4) location characteristics. Data are available for 2,438 students and 686 community colleges.

Despite the detailed institutional measures utilized, Bailey et al. (2005) conclude that institutional factors offer little explanatory power once individual student characteristics are controlled for. By way of explanation, they offer four suggestions. First, they note that individual variables are measured with more precision than institutional variables, an especially important point when outcome variables are measured at the individual student level. Second, it is probably not too surprising that well-prepared students backed by adequate financial resources are likely to do well in a variety of institutions. On the other hand, students facing academic challenges or those with heavy financial responsibilities may run into difficulties even in strongly academically oriented colleges. Third, the authors note that individual student success is likely to be more strongly influenced by "subcultures" within a college than by the average characteristics of the entire institution. Finally, they point out that measured institutional characteristics do not capture effective institutional policies such as pedagogic strategies, guidance and academic counseling efforts, faculty culture, and differences in organization.

In the next section, we examine in greater depth the role of institutional factors in determining the academic success of Latino and Asian students.

Explanation of Observed Race/Ethnicity Gaps

For male and female students and all three outcome variables, Table 5.8 compares the observed, or unadjusted gaps, by race or ethnicity with the regression-adjusted gaps. The observed gaps are calculated from Table 5.2, and the regression-adjusted gaps are parameter estimates obtained for race or ethnicity variables in the regressions underlying Tables 5.6 and 5.7. Beginning with the AA degree, we noted earlier that receipt of an AA is a less common outcome than transferring, and that race/ethnicity differences in AA degree receipt tend to be small. Table 5.8 indicates that already small observed gaps are reduced to essentially zero in the three male relationships and in the female black-white comparison. The positive observed gap favoring Asian over white women is cut by roughly two-thirds, and the small negative gap favoring white over Latino women reverses sign.

Turning to total credits earned, controlling for differences in the explanatory variables likewise has the effect of substantially reducing in size positive observed race/ethnicity gaps for Asians and negative observed gaps for blacks. This result holds for both male and female students. For female Asians, for example, an observed gap of nearly 10 credits is reduced to only 2.6 credits. Among Latinos, the small negative gaps favoring whites in total credits earned are seen to actually reverse sign once adjustment has been made for differences in the explanatory variables.

For the transfer relationships, much the same story can be told for Latino and black students. That is, Table 5.8 shows that controlling for differences in our explanatory variables is sufficient to substantially reduce the size of negative Latino-white gaps and to entirely eliminate the negative black-white gaps. For Asian students, on the other hand, we

Table 5.8 Comparison of Unadjusted and Regression-Adjusted Gaps by Race or Ethnicity in Educational Outcome Variables, by Gender

Outcome variable	Latino-white	Black-white	Asian-white
	Males		
Transfer			
Unadjusted	−0.075	−0.054	0.105
Adjusted	−0.021**	−0.007	0.074**
AA degree			
Unadjusted	−0.024	−0.029	0.026
Adjusted	0.004	0.000	0.006
Total credits			
Unadjusted	−3.10	−7.6	10.7
Adjusted	1.87**	−3.14**	4.02**
	Females		
Transfer			
Unadjusted	−0.073	−0.074	0.114
Adjusted	−0.020**	−0.001	0.088**
AA degree			
Unadjusted	−0.022	−0.052	0.040
Adjusted	0.012**	−0.002	0.014**
Total credits			
Unadjusted	−0.9	−8.1	9.9
Adjusted	3.02**	−2.26**	2.60**

NOTE: **Indicates regression estimate statistically significant at the 0.05 level.

are much less successful in explaining observed gaps favoring Asians over whites. After controlling for all five categories of explanatory variables, we reduce the male gap from 10.5 percentage points to 7.4 percentage points, a reduction of only about 30 percent. The reduction in the slightly larger gap for female students is even smaller at about 23 percent.

Table 5.9 reports "explained" portions, or differentials, of observed race/ethnicity gaps in student transfers and total credits earned based on the standard decomposition approach first described in Oaxaca (1973). Conceptually, explained differentials are the flip side of the regression-adjusted, or unexplained, gaps shown in the previous table that remain after controlling for differences in explanatory variables.[6] In turn, explained differentials are decomposed in Table 5.9 into the individual contributions of each of our five categories of explanatory variables. We do not report the results for AA degree receipt because of the small size of observed differentials.

To clarify the interpretation of Table 5.9, consider, for example, estimates for the differential between Latino and white males in student transfers. The table indicates that we can explain about 72 percent (= 0.054 / 0.075) of the observed gap in transfer rates by controlling for differences in our explanatory variables. Of the explained differential of 5.4 percentage points, by far the most important category of explanatory variables is the set of community college progress variables. This category of explanatory variables accounts for about 70 percent of the explained differential or 51 percent of the observed differential. That is, Latino males lag behind white males in transferring to four-year institutions primarily because they fail to match whites in terms of academic progress. Other results appearing in the table indicate that we can reach much the same conclusion for Latino males in the credits earned relationship, Latino females in the transfer and credits earned relationships, and both black males and black females in the transfer and credits earned relationships.

Table 5.9 suggests a quite different situation for Asian students. As indicated earlier, we do a much less satisfactory job in explaining observed differentials in transfer rates for Asians. As a proportion of observed differentials, the explained differential is only 42 percent for males and 39 percent for females. Among male students, Asian-white differences in background variables and financial need are shown to

Table 5.9 Decomposition of "Explained" Differentials by Race or Ethnicity in Student Transfers and Total Credits Earned, by Gender

Gaps in outcome variable	Latino-white	Black-white	Asian-white
	Males		
Transfer			
Explained gap (total)	0.054	0.051	0.044
Background variables	−0.002	0.003	0.012
Financial need	0.003	−0.002	0.018
Educational goals	0.003	−0.001	0.006
Community college progress	0.038	0.041	0.003
Institutional variables	0.012	0.009	0.005
Explained gap/observed gap	0.72	0.94	0.42
Total credits			
Explained gap (total)	4.45	4.52	7.77
Background variables	−0.94	0.56	3.59
Financial need	1.11	−0.48	3.61
Educational goals	0.28	−0.07	0.34
Community college progress	3.81	4.50	−0.01
Institutional variables	0.19	0.02	0.25
Explained gap/observed gap	1.44	0.59	0.73
	Females		
Transfer			
Explained gap (total)	0.052	0.077	0.044
Background variables	0.001	0.003	0.007
Financial need	−0.003	−0.002	−0.003
Educational goals	0.002	0.002	0.002
Community college progress	0.039	0.062	0.039
Institutional variables	0.014	0.013	0.014
Explained gap/observed gap	0.71	1.04	0.39
Total credits			
Explained gap	3.35	5.77	8.20
Background variables	−0.86	0.93	4.12
Financial need	0.16	−0.93	2.76
Educational goals	0.18	0.09	0.30
Community college progress	4.05	5.97	0.79
Institutional variables	−0.17	−0.29	0.23
Explained gap/observed gap	3.72	0.71	0.83

NOTE: Negative observed and explained differentials for Latinos and blacks are treated as positive to allow more ready comparison with Asians differentials. Used in the decompositions are pooled parameter estimates from regressions omitting race or ethnicity variables.

be the most important considerations in explaining the relatively small explained differential. On the other hand, superior community college academic performance is the most important factor for female students. We do a much better job of explaining observed Asian-white gaps in total credits earned. Table 5.9 shows that the leading categories of explanatory variables for both men and women are background variables and financial need.

ADDITIONAL RESULTS FOR EDUCATIONAL OUTCOMES

First-Generation Immigrants

First-time-freshmen data allow us to hone in on first-generation immigrants using our measures of foreign high school diploma and citizenship. With these variables, we define first-generation immigrants as students possessing a foreign high school diploma, plus students who are not U.S. citizens and do not possess a foreign high school diploma. Educational outcomes and selected personal attributes of these individuals broken down by gender and race/ethnicity are displayed in Table 5.10. To sharpen the comparisons, we include for Latinos and Asians means calculated for nonimmigrant as well as immigrant students. For whites and blacks, we include only first-generation immigrant students. First-generation immigrants total 32,810 males and 33,465 females. Hence, we classify about 22 percent of both male and female students enrolled in CCCS colleges as first-generation immigrants.

The totals appearing in Table 5.10 probably underestimate the true number of first-generation immigrant students. Left out are foreign-born individuals who, before enrolling in a community college, came to the United States without a high school degree and subsequently became citizens. On the other hand, there is reason to think that we may overstate the number of first-generation immigrants. Adding together the two non-citizen categories under the heading Citizenship Status, Table 5.10 shows that 90–95 percent of first-generation immigrant students are noncitizens. The remaining 5–10 percent must then be United States citizens who possess a foreign high school diploma. While we believe that most of these individuals came to this country as immigrants and later became citizens, it is also possible that others were born in the United States and received a foreign high school diploma in a student-exchange program.

The personal characteristics of first-generation immigrant students described in Table 5.10 indicate three basic differences from the characteristics of all CCCS students. First, as expected, first-generation immigrant students are distinctly more likely to be Latino and Asian. Latinos and Asians each represent about 40 percent of all first-generation immigrant students. By comparison, Latino and Asian students as a percentage of all students are about 30 percent and 15 percent, respectively. Slightly over 30 percent of all Latino students are first-generation immigrants, while nearly 60 percent of all Asian students are first-generation immigrants. A second difference, also expected, is that first-generation immigrants are more likely to lack English language skills and to take more basic skills courses while attending a community college.

The third difference between first-generation immigrant students and all students is age. First-generation immigrants are distinctly older than other students in the same race/ethnicity categories. Among Latino males, for example, over 46 percent of first-generation immigrant students are older than 25, as opposed to about 29 percent of all students and 20 percent of nonimmigrants. A striking finding is that about two-thirds of white males who are first-generation immigrants are older than 25. About 60 percent of white female first-generation immigrants fall into the older age category.

Based on the regression results in Tables 5.6 and 5.7, older students are expected, other things equal, to have a less successful community college experience. This is exactly what we find for whites and especially for Latinos. Again looking at Latino males, Table 5.10 shows that the transfer rate drops from 8.5 percent for nonimmigrant students to 5.0 percent for first-generation immigrant students. The effect of an older age for first-generation immigrant Latinos is reinforced by the negative effects of a higher proportion of high school dropouts, a lighter average class load, and less initial student interest in transferring.

Among blacks, on the other hand, outcome measures are consistently higher among the small number of first-generation immigrant students than for all black students, a result that holds for both males and females. For example, black female first-generation immigrants earn on average 30.5 credits, as opposed to 20.0 credits completed for all female black students (see Table 5.2). It is interesting to note that black male first-generation immigrants enjoy higher outcomes than immigrant white males on all three outcome measures. For first-generation immigrant black females, we report a higher AA degree rate than for immigrant white females.

For Asians, differences in educational outcome measures between first-generation immigrant students and nonimmigrant students are small, and the sign of the differences vary by outcome measure. For both male and female Asian students, first-generation immigrants earn AA degrees at a slightly higher rate and complete more total credits. On the other hand, the transfer rate of first-generation immigrants falls short of the rate of nonimmigrants. Among Asian females, for example, the transfer rate for first-generation immigrant students is 24.4 percent as compared to 32.7 percent for nonimmigrants. There is little difference in the educational goals of Asian first-generation immigrants and nonimmigrants.

Overall, just as is the case for all students, Table 5.10 indicates that the performance of first-generation Asian immigrants substantially exceeds that of first-generation immigrants in the other race or ethnicity categories. Conversely, first-generation immigrant Latino students lag behind other first-generation immigrant students and Latino nonimmigrants. It is instructive to compare these findings with those of Leinbach and Bailey (2006) for Latino students in the CUNY system in New York City. Leinbach and Bailey find, as we do, that Latino immigrants accumulate far fewer total credits than other immigrants, keeping in mind that they measure total credits across both two-year and four-year colleges.[7] Total credits earned is very similar for immigrant and native-born Latino students. In contrast to our results, Leinbach and Bailey find that the AA degree rate is essentially the same for Latino and other immigrant students (at about 20 percent), and that the transfer rate of other immigrants (about 15 percent) only slightly exceeds the rate of Latino immigrants. Nevertheless, Latino immigrants are far less likely than other immigrant students to eventually earn a bachelor's degree. We report that Latinos lag substantially behind other immigrants in terms of both AA degree rate and transfer rate. As seen in Table 5.10, the AA degree rate for Latino male immigrants is 4.6 percent as compared to 11.6 percent for Asian males, and transfer rates for Latino and Asian males are 5.0 percent and 23.4 percent, respectively.

Table 5.10 Descriptive Statistics for Outcome Variables and Selected Explanatory Variables for White and Black First-Generation Immigrant Students and for Latino and Asian First-Generation Immigrant and Nonimmigrant Students, by Gender

Variable	Latinos		Males		Asians[a]	
	Immigrants	Non-immigrants	Whites	Blacks	Immigrants	Non-immigrants
Outcomes						
Transfer	0.050	0.085	0.114	0.141	0.234	0.280
AA degree	0.046	0.061	0.056	0.087	0.116	0.095
Total credits earned	19.6	22.9	20.8	25.1	37.6	32.9
Educational background						
Foreign high school diploma	0.200	—	0.259	0.306	0.355	—
GED	0.049	0.070	0.017	0.035	0.023	0.043
No high school diploma	0.217	0.121	0.035	0.017	0.091	0.072
Took/needs ESL	0.254	0.034	0.099	0.107	0.299	0.079
Basic skills courses ratio	0.281	0.123	0.083	0.111	0.164	0.077
Citizenship status						
Permanent resident	0.770	—	0.376	0.408	0.685	—
Other	0.184	—	0.557	0.509	0.257	—
Financial need						
Age 26–60	0.462	0.202	0.665	0.556	0.284	0.158
Credits attempted/semester	6.13	7.25	5.28	6.48	8.47	8.11
Educational goals						
Transferring	0.202	0.343	0.207	0.330	0.437	0.439

			Females			
Occupational skills	0.331	0.299	0.160	0.189	0.174	0.167
Educational development	0.178	0.076	0.084	0.068	0.114	0.088
Number of students	13,504	28,566	5,791	1,083	12,432	9,525
Percent of total immigrants	41.2	—	17.6	3.3	37.9	—
Immigrants/all students	0.321	—	0.091	0.075	0.566	—
Outcomes						
Transfer	0.060	0.103	0.159	0.107	0.244	0.327
AA degree	0.076	0.104	0.115	0.126	0.169	0.141
Total credits earned	25.9	27.8	33.5	30.5	40.1	34.8
Educational background						
Foreign high school diploma	0.211	—	0.505	0.357	0.403	—
GED	0.045	0.059	0.024	0.055	0.016	0.032
No high school diploma	0.205	0.111	0.046	0.084	0.081	0.071
Took/needs ESL	0.295	0.040	0.212	0.115	0.346	0.108
Basic skills courses ratio	0.330	0.142	0.162	0.168	0.194	0.088
Citizenship status						
Permanent resident	0.810	—	0.607	0.459	0.683	—
Other	0.133	—	0.292	0.439	0.242	—
Financial need						
Age 26–60	0.462	0.225	0.597	0.520	0.347	0.201
Credits attempted/semester	6.24	7.42	7.26	7.15	8.12	7.85

(continued)

Table 5.10 (continued)

| | Latinos | | | | Asians[a] | |
	Immigrants	Non-immigrants	Whites	Blacks	Immigrants	Non-immigrants
			Females			
Educational goals						
Transferring	0.210	0.355	0.264	0.304	0.399	0.418
Occupational skills	0.301	0.273	0.264	0.300	0.176	0.158
Educational development	0.212	0.077	0.178	0.081	0.146	0.105
Number of students	13,970	31,992	5,145	954	13,396	8,835
Percent of total immigrants	41.7	—	15.4	2.9	40.0	—
Immigrants/all students	0.304	—	0.078	0.058	0.603	—

NOTE: First-generation immigrants are defined as students with a foreign high school diploma or as non-U.S. citizens who do not possess a foreign high school diploma. A dash (—) indicates variables not calculated for nonimmigrants.

[a] Includes Filipinos.

Later in this section, we look for differences between community college campuses in seeking to explain the higher transfer rate of Asian students and the lower rate of Latinos. In Chapter 6, we exploit the finer two-digit breakdown of ethnicity available for Asians and Latinos to gain further insight into the contrasting educational outcomes for Asians and Latinos.

High School Dropouts

A second student group of particular interest is high school dropouts. We focus on high school dropouts for two reasons. First, community colleges represent an important "second-chance" opportunity for dropouts to obtain the academic background or occupational skills necessary to continue their education or to enter the mainstream labor force. Second, since students can enter community colleges without a high school diploma, there is concern in California and other states that the number of community college students who are high school dropouts will expand substantially as students fail to complete high school because of state exit exams. In California, this exam is called the California High School Exit Exam.

Before enrolling in a community college, it is common for U.S. high school dropouts to earn a GED certificate. As noted in Appendix A, information on whether students have passed a GED exam is included in the FTF Cohort File. This is significant because this file contains information collected from students at the time of first enrollment. Since high school dropouts may or may not have earned a GED prior to entering a community college, we include both categories of dropouts in the descriptive statistics, again stratified by gender and race/ethnicity, shown in Table 5.11. Note how common a GED is for students we characterize as high school dropouts. Between one-third and one-half of white and black students who dropped out of high school earned a GED. This is not too surprising as the GED is a uniquely U.S. educational certificate. But even for Latinos and Asians, individuals much more likely to be first-generation immigrants than whites and blacks, GED recipients are between 23 and 29 percent of students who dropped out of high school. Overall, about 16 percent of male and female students are classified as high school dropouts. Latino students are overrepresented among dropouts, while whites and Asians are underrepresented. Dropouts represent

21.5 percent and 19.5 percent of all Latino male and female students, respectively.

Comparing students who are high school dropouts in Table 5.11 to all community college students in Table 5.2, the most striking finding is the low level of educational outcomes for dropouts. Even Asian dropouts, who again report relatively high outcomes in comparison to other race/ethnicity groups in Table 5.11, do more poorly relative to other Asian students including first-generation immigrants. For example, the transfer rate of Asian male dropouts is only 9.9 percent as compared to 25.4 percent for all Asian males and 23.4 percent for Asian first-generation immigrant males. Among Latino dropouts, the transfer rate is a miniscule 2–3 percent, which is matched by an equally low AA degree receipt rate. Credits earned by Latino dropouts average only about half the number of credits earned by all Latino students, both male and female.

The lack of success as measured by our educational outcome variables is consistent with the individual attributes of dropout students described in Table 5.11. Compared to all students, dropouts across all four race/ethnicity categories tend to be older, take a higher ratio of basic skills courses, and attempt fewer credits per semester. Furthermore, dropouts are less interested in ultimately transferring and more interested in acquiring occupational skills and educational development. Among the community college progress variables shown, dropouts tend to complete fewer courses of those they attempt and take fewer courses that are transferable. The GPA of dropouts is not noticeably different from that of all students in the same race/ethnicity category. What is different is the large fraction of dropouts for which GPA is missing, indicating students enrolled in only nongraded courses. For example, over 31 percent of Latino male dropout students took no courses at all for a grade.

To the extent that an increased enrollment of high school dropouts materializes in the CCCS, these findings indicate that California community colleges should be prepared to redirect additional resources to their basic skills curriculums. Our results also suggest that community colleges may need to increase their counseling and mentoring efforts to encourage dropout students to raise their educational aspirations.

Table 5.11 Descriptive Statistics for Outcome Variables and Selected Explanatory Variables for High School Dropouts, by Gender and One-Digit Race or Ethnicity

Variable	Latinos	Whites	Blacks	Asians[a]
		Males		
Educational outcome				
Transfer	0.023	0.047	0.033	0.099
Receipt of AA degree	0.019	0.032	0.017	0.050
Total credits earned	11.5	12.8	9.6	22.3
Educational background				
GED	0.294	0.507	0.418	0.277
Took or needs ESL	0.191	0.009	0.013	0.249
Basic skills courses/all courses	0.259	0.093	0.152	0.209
Citizenship status				
Permanent resident	0.349	0.024	0.020	0.455
Other	0.048	0.010	0.018	0.112
Financial need				
Age 26–60	0.479	0.460	0.392	0.316
Credits attempted/semester	5.69	6.12	7.09	7.04
Educational goals				
Transferring	0.140	0.208	0.254	0.288
Occupational skills	0.410	0.386	0.346	0.222
Educational development	0.201	0.127	0.163	0.176
Community college progress variables				
GPA	2.02	2.13	1.79	2.03
GPA missing	0.314	0.220	0.299	0.205
Credits earned ratio	0.455	0.476	0.319	0.472
Transferable courses ratio	0.238	0.341	0.375	0.348
Number of students	9,054	8,813	3,016	2,516
Percent of total dropouts	38.7	37.6	12.9	10.8
		Females		
Educational outcome				
Transfer	0.025	0.056	0.030	0.127
Receipt of AA degree	0.034	0.054	0.032	0.092
Total credits earned	15.4	16.2	12.6	25.5
Educational background				
GED	0.282	0.462	0.359	0.226
Took or needs ESL	0.229	0.012	0.012	0.327

(continued)

Table 5.11 (continued)

Variable	Latinos	Whites	Blacks	Asians[a]
		Females		
Citizenship status				
Permanent resident	0.351	0.026	0.017	0.491
Other	0.040	0.014	0.021	0.097
Financial need				
Age 26–60	0.568	0.555	0.459	0.442
Credits attempted/semester	5.9	6.2	7.5	6.7
Educational goals				
Transferring	0.131	0.186	0.193	0.249
Occupational skills	0.364	0.364	0.379	0.207
Educational development	0.233	0.130	0.185	0.229
Community college progress variables				
GPA	2.14	2.26	1.79	2.32
GPA missing	0.287	0.201	0.279	0.223
Credits earned ratio	0.497	0.499	0.324	0.562
Transferable courses ratio	0.253	0.367	0.313	0.328
Number of students	8,951	8,912	3,434	2,217
Percent of total dropouts	38.1	37.9	14.6	9.4

NOTE: High school dropouts include GED recipients.
[a] Includes Filipinos.

The Effect of Clustering on Institution-Specific Transfer Rates

In the second section of this chapter, we described that once we controlled for the effects of a variety of student-level characteristics, the inclusion of six college-specific explanatory variables had little effect on estimated race or ethnicity effects in the transfer, AA receipt, and total credits earned equations. Nor, for that matter, does the inclusion of institutional variables affect measurably the coefficients estimated for the student-level explanatory variables. Because FTF data provide information on the college initially attended by each student, an available alternative approach to including college-specific explanatory variables is to estimate a relationship that includes dummy variables for each of the 106 CCCS colleges. Supporting this "fixed-effects" approach is the suggestion of Bailey et al. (2005) that measured college-specific characteristics may not capture unobserved, but still important, variables such as specific institutional policies that affect program completion.

Following up on the fixed-effects approach, we estimated separate transfer regressions for males and females. Two main results were obtained. First, estimated race/ethnicity gaps in transfer rates are not changed substantially from those shown in Table 5.8. That is, regardless of college attended, Asians appear to transfer at a higher rate than whites, and whites at a higher rate than Latinos. Second, controlling for student-level variables, college fixed-effect estimates are frequently quite large, often exceeding 5 percentage points and occasionally exceeding 10 percentage points.

There is some support in the literature for the second of these results. In a study summarized in Chapter 3, Ehrenberg and Smith (2004) report evidence of large community college-specific effects on transfer propensity and attainment of a BA degree, although they indicate that these effects often disappear once student characteristics are controlled for. Bailey et al. (2006) find that community colleges differ in their effectiveness in helping students graduate, even after controlling for characteristics of the student body.

Based on our evidence showing large college fixed effects, we wondered whether, controlling for individual student characteristics, particular campuses are especially effective, or especially ineffective, in promoting transfers to four-year colleges of their Latino and Asian students. To answer this question, we stratified our data by the one-digit level of race/ethnicity (using data for both males and females) to estimate college-specific fixed effects in separate regressions for Latinos, whites, blacks, and Asians. For each race/ethnicity category, frequency distributions of the 105 college fixed effects estimated are shown in Table 5.12. To clarify the interpretation of these estimates, consider, for example, the first row of the distribution shown for whites. The number 3 appearing in that cell indicates that, after controlling for our individual-level explanatory variables, a total of 3 (out of 105) colleges are found to have an adjusted transfer rate that is 12 percentage points or higher above the transfer rate calculated for whites attending the reference college. (College number 106, Victor Valley Community College, serves as the reference category college.)

Looking across race/ethnicity categories in Table 5.12, the spread of the distribution estimated for Latinos is clearly smaller than the spreads

Table 5.12   Frequency Distributions of Estimates of College-Specific Fixed Effects on Transfer Rates, Holding Constant Student-Level Characteristics, by One-Digit Race or Ethnicity

Percentage point difference from reference college[a]	Latinos	Whites	Blacks	Asians
12.0 or higher	1	3	2	9
9.0 to 11.9	2	3	1	7
6.0 to 8.9	4	9	8	18
3.0 to 5.9	12	20	13	18
0 to 2.9	40	45	38	22
−0.1 to −2.9	37	8	33	14
−3.0 to −5.9	7	13	4	7
−6.0 to −8.9	2	4	4	5
−9.0 or lower	0	0	2	5
Transfer rate for reference college (in percent)	7.3	12.7	9.0	21.6
Number of colleges	105	105	105	105

[a] The reference college is Victor Valley. For the dummy explanatory variables, held constant in this calculation is age 25 or younger, U.S. high school diploma, U.S. citizen, does not need/took ESL, and undecided educational goal. For the continuous explanatory variables, we use race/ethnicity-specific means.

for whites and blacks, and the spread of the Asian distribution is larger still. But even for Latinos, substantial variability is indicated. Notice from the Latino distribution that standardized transfer rates for 28 colleges are at least 3 percent higher or at least 3 percent lower than that for the reference college.

We next sought to determine whether a large concentration of students of a particular race or ethnicity background has an impact on the standardized transfer rate measured for that race/ethnicity category across the 106 CCCS colleges in our data set. Table 5.13 presents separate regression estimates for Latinos and Asians. Concentration or "clustering" is measured by the ratio of students of a particular ethnic background to all students, and the dependent variable is the ethnicity-specific standardized transfer rate calculated for each campus. Control variables in columns (1) and (3) are proximity of the community college to nearest UC campus and nearest CSU campus and total enrollment. Close proximity may make it possible for 1) students to transfer

Table 5.13 OLS Estimates of Effects of College-Level Explanatory Variables on College-Specific Transfer Rates Calculated Holding Constant Individual Student Characteristics, Latino and Asian Students

College-level variable	Latinos		Asians	
	(1)	(2)	(3)	(4)
Constant	9.55**	8.52**	20.58**	18.17**
	(1.47)	(1.87)	(2.57)	(2.95)
Ratio of Latino students to all students	−8.12**	−7.79**	—	—
	(2.82)	(2.85)	—	—
Ratio of Asian students to all students	—	—	23.45**	20.48**
			(7.63)	(7.78)
Total students (in thousands)	0.026	0.042	0.096	0.150
	(0.063)	(0.066)	(0.106)	(0.110)
Distance from UC (in miles)	0.003	0.005	−0.009	−0.004
	(0.012)	(0.012)	(0.020)	(0.002)
Distance from CSU (in miles)	0.008	0.013	0.009	0.022
	(0.021)	(0.021)	(0.035)	(0.035)
Multiple campus district	—	0.90	—	2.76
		(1.00)		(1.69)
R^2	0.082	0.089	0.135	0.157
Mean of dependent variable	8.23	8.23	24.84	24.84

NOTE:**Statistically significant at the 0.05 level. A dash (—) indicates variable not included in the regression. $N = 106$; standard errors in parentheses.

without having to move their households, and 2) development of closer relationships between faculty and administrators of two-year and four-year colleges, allowing a more seamless transfer process. Total enrollment is included to capture the scale required for a community college to develop specialized programs designed to assist particular categories of students. In columns (2) and (4), we add a dummy variable measuring whether a community college is a member of a multicampus community college district. Multicampus districts typically serve large metropolitan areas.[8] These control variables are discussed in detail in Gill and Leigh (2004).

As indicated in Table 5.13, coefficients estimated for our control variables are not typically statistically significant, and the R^2 statistics are quite low. Nevertheless, we obtain a striking result for our clustering variables. Columns (1) and (2) suggest that a greater concentration of Latino students has a negative and statistically significant impact on the standardized transfer rate. On the other hand, columns (3) and (4) show that clustering of Asian students has a positive, and even larger, impact on standardized transfer rates. In terms of magnitudes, a 10-percentage-point increase in the share of Latino students decreases the standardized transfer rate for Latinos by nearly 1 percentage point. The same 10-percentage-point increase in the share of Asians increases the standardized Asian transfer rate by 2.0 to 2.3 percentage points.

It is common in the literature to find that share of minority students affects a community college's transfer rate, with the Latino share typically depressing transfers and the Asian share increasing transfers. For example, Wassmer, Moore, and Shulock (2004) find these Latino and Asian effects for California community colleges. There are two important differences between our results and those reported by Wassmer, Moore, and Shulock. First, their study is based on college-level data. Although they attempt to control for student body characteristics, their control variables measured at the college level are likely to be imperfect measures of individual student characteristics. Hence, their finding for Latinos might simply indicate that admitting a larger proportion of less-well-prepared students results in less favorable educational outcomes. In contrast, our dependent variable, the standardized transfer rate, is purged of individual student characteristics that might lead to cross-college differences. Second, our dependent variable is the college's ethnicity-specific transfer rate rather than the college's overall transfer rate. Hence, our results establish that, after controlling for differences between students that affect their transfer propensity, a college's share of Latinos depresses the Latino transfer rate, while a greater share of Asians, again controlling for individual student characteristics, increases the Asian transfer rate.

How can we explain these diametrically opposite effects for Latinos and Asians? One possibility is that the clustering variables capture differences in socioeconomic backgrounds, with the Latino variable representing a less advantaged background and the Asian variable a more advantaged background. Data from the 2000 census (U.S. Census 2000) indicate for California that there are large differences in median family income stratified by one-digit race/ethnicity categories.[9] What jumps out from these data are enormous differences in incomes between Latino families and white and Asian families. Specifically, median family incomes in 1999 for Asians and whites are about $61,400 and $60,200, respectively, as compared to about $36,000 for Latinos. Median family income for blacks is about $39,700.

These large differences, nevertheless, probably overstate income differences that would be observed for the families of community college students, since high-income Asian and white families are more likely to send their children to UC and CSU campuses than to a community college. In the absence of student-level data on variables such as family income and parents' education, what we have done is to develop measures at the college level of median family income and average education in the community (see Table 5.5). But, as discussed earlier in this chapter, we were unable to find much of an impact of these college-level variables on our educational outcome measures.

Another possible explanation of particular relevance to students who are immigrants is Borjas's (1999, pp. 55–58) suggestion that the geographic clustering of immigrant groups in ethnic enclaves has an important effect on labor market outcomes, in either a positive or negative direction. As Borjas explains, a positive clustering effect might arise because the "warm embrace" of the enclave helps immigrants escape the labor market discrimination that they would otherwise encounter. On the other hand, clustering may hinder movement to better-paying jobs outside the enclave by reducing immigrants' incentive to learn the culture and language of the American labor market.

In an education context, clustering of immigrant groups in particular colleges may affect educational outcomes, either positively or negatively, for similar reasons. That is, the presence of a substantial number of students of a particular racial or ethnic background may supply a new student of the same background with the support system needed to succeed in an unfamiliar environment. Note that we are emphasizing that it is the share of students of the same race or ethnicity that is important. Our results for a limited set of institutional-specific variables coupled with similar evidence supplied by Bailey et al. (2005) for a broader set of such variables suggest that a college's overall academic culture has little impact. On the other hand, clustering may inhibit students from expanding their educational aspirations beyond the norms established by their peer group, where peer group is defined in terms of students of the same race/ethnicity background. Note that what we mean by educational aspirations must go beyond educational goals such as a student's intention to transfer, since these goals are held constant in our analysis.

Proceeding with this argument, a Latino student attending a college with few other Latinos is obliged to interact with students of other race/ethnicity backgrounds. If they are white or Asian, these students are likely to place a greater value on educational attainment than is the case in the Latino community. Relevant here is the discussion of "Hispanic culture" in Chapter 3. As described by Wassmer, Moore, and Shulock (2004), the idea is that while individual Latino parents value the education of their children, the broader culture places a higher value on family welfare than on individual aspirations and encourages Latino youth to stay close to home and family. Lazear (2005) makes much the same point in a labor market context, arguing that because they tend to live in ethnic enclaves, Mexican immigrants are slower to assimilate, earn lower wages, and complete fewer years of education.

For Asians, the argument goes in just the opposite direction. That is, clustering results in Asian students who come to college with high aspirations finding reinforcement by interacting with students with similarly high aspirations. In colleges in which the concentration of Asians is low, however, the high aspirations of Asian students may be diminished by interaction with students of other racial/ethnic backgrounds with generally lower aspirations.

We return to this argument in the next chapter when we disaggregate Latino and Asian students by national or regional origin. As will be shown, subgroups of Latinos and Asians differ in a variety of ways, including the proportion of first-generation immigrant students.

SUMMARY

We began this chapter with a detailed overview of the data that are available for FTF students enrolled in CCCS campuses during the 1996–1997 academic year. Focusing on our three community college outcome variables, we then identified important gaps between Latino and white students and between Asian and white students. Observed gaps favor whites over Latinos and Asians over whites. We also pointed out a number of differences by race or ethnicity in our student-level and college-level explanatory variables that might be important in understanding these gaps in educational outcomes.

Next we proceeded with a quantitative analysis designed to identify barriers to educational attainment for Latino students, and, for Asians, to identify factors that lead to their superior academic performance. We were quite successful in explaining the gaps favoring whites over Latinos. Looking at transferring to a four-year college, for example, we were able to reduce the observed male Latino-white gap of 7.5 percentage points to a standardized gap of only 2 percentage points. Our decomposition analysis indicates that the primary factor in explaining the observed Latino-white gap is failure to keep up with white students in terms of academic progress.

On the other hand, our ability to explain Asian-white gaps in educational outcomes was mixed. While we are reasonably successful in explaining the observed gaps in receipt of an AA degree and total credits earned, we were less successful in accounting for the gap in transfers. Among Asian females, for example, our regression-adjusted gap of 8.8 percentage points is only marginally smaller than the observed gap of 11.4 percentage points.

We also attempted to hone in on two student categories of particular interest to policymakers: first-generation immigrants and high school dropouts. First-generation immigrants represent about 32 percent and 57 percent, respectively, of all Latino and Asian students. Probably our most important finding for recent immigrants is that the academic success of Asian immigrants far exceeds that of other immigrant groups and is comparable to that of Asian nonimmigrants. On the other hand, first-generation Latino immigrants do less well than other immigrant groups and Latino nonimmigrants.

High school dropouts represent about 16 percent of all community college students. Our cross-tabulations indicate that dropouts are distinctly older than other students and are disproportionately Latino. Not surprisingly, dropouts perform very poorly as measured by our three outcome variables. For example, the observed transfer rate for Latino male dropouts is a miniscule 2.3 percent. Even the 9.9 percent rate observed for Asian males is far below the 23.4 percent reported by Asian male first-generation immigrants.

Finally, we explored more deeply the question of whether individual colleges might have different effects on educational outcomes. Taking a college fixed-effects approach, an affirmative answer to this question led us to wonder whether, controlling for individual student characteristics, particular campuses are especially effective, or especially ineffective, in promoting student transfers of their Latino and Asian students. Measured across colleges, we presented evidence indicating that a concentration, or "clustering," of Latino students decreases the transfer rate of Latinos adjusted for differences in student characteristics. At the same time, a clustering of Asian students appears to increase the transfer rate of Asians. We return to this finding in the next chapter.

Notes

1. Appendix A suggests a fourth community college outcome variable that might be considered: receipt of an occupational skills certificate. As indicated in Table A.1, however, only 3 percent of students earned a certificate. Furthermore, as the table shows, certificates are awarded in programs that differ substantially in terms of number of semester credits required. If we decided to focus on certificates awarded on completion of 30–59 semester credits, for example, only 1.2 percent of students received a certificate.
2. As indicated in Appendix A, FTF data distinguish transferable courses as transferable to both UC and CSU campuses or transferable to CSU campuses only. Our conversations with Charles Klein, a specialist in student transfers in the Curriculum Standards and Instruction Services unit in the Chancellor's Office, indicate that the community colleges themselves determine which courses are transferable to CSUs, while the UC system scrutinizes all courses it designates as transferable. Consequently, we define transferable courses as courses transferable to both UCs and CSUs in our analysis.
3. We also pursued a sequential estimation approach beginning by controlling for background characteristics, then adding financial need variables, then educational goals, then community college progress measures, and, finally, college-level variables. These estimates are referred to later in this section.
4. We also estimated some of our models using logistic regression. In general, the marginal effects obtained from the logistic regressions are little changed from the OLS estimates reported in the Tables 5.6 and 5.7.
5. To investigate whether the effects of our background variables differ across race/ethnicity categories, we interacted measures of foreign high school, ESL, and permanent resident and other citizenship with race/ethnicity dummy variables. We were specifically looking for evidence of differential effects of these variables for Latinos and Asians. What we found, however, is that the Latino and

Asian interaction terms are generally small and insignificant. In the few cases in which the coefficients estimated are statistically significant, they are of the same sign. The strongest interaction effects are found for black students, with the evidence indicating that blacks who attended high school in other countries and who are not citizens enjoy superior community college outcomes in comparison to other blacks. As will be seen, this result is consistent with our findings later in this chapter for first-generation black students.

6. The explained differentials appearing in Table 5.9 differ slightly from comparable estimates calculated as the differences between unadjusted gaps and regression-adjusted gaps in Table 5.8. The reason is that the regression-adjusted estimates in Table 5.8 are parameter estimates obtained for the race or ethnicity variables. Hence, they measure shifts in the regression functions for students who differ by race or ethnicity. In contrast, the explained differentials shown in Table 5.9 are calculated as differences by race or ethnicity in student characteristics and college-level measures, which are weighted by parameter estimates obtained from a pooled regression that omits race/ethnicity variables. In other words, estimates in Table 5.8 measure shifts in the regression function for students who differ by race or ethnicity. The Table 5.9 estimates capture race/ethnicity shifts in the regression function plus differences between pooled coefficient estimates and race/ethnicity-specific coefficient estimates.

7. Although Leinbach and Bailey (2006) do not emphasize Asian students, they do note that Asians, both immigrants and native-born, have significantly higher mean credits earned than any other subpopulation distinguished by race/ethnicity and nativity.

8. Whether a community college comprises its own district or is part of a multi-campus district is an important part of the analysis in Chapter 7 concerning how well community colleges respond to local labor market demand.

9. As will be seen in Chapter 6, median family income calculated for all Latinos and all Asians masks substantial differences within these broad ethnicity categories.

6

Responsiveness to the Educational Needs of Immigrants by Narrowly Defined Ethnic Categories

In this chapter, we continue our analysis begun in Chapter 5 that attempts to explain observed gaps in community college outcome variables for Latino and Asian students. As discussed in Chapter 5, Asian community college students outperform whites despite disadvantages associated with a high proportion of recent immigrants. At the same time, Latinos, who must contend with similar disadvantages, tend to lag behind whites. When we isolated on first-generation immigrant students, in addition, outcome measures are found to be much lower for Latino students than for other immigrants. In contrast, educational outcomes for first-generation Asian immigrants not only exceed those for other first-generation immigrants, but they are comparable to those for nonimmigrant Asians.

The innovation in this chapter is that the analysis is carried out at the level of narrowly defined, or two-digit, ethnicity categories specified in FTF data for Latinos and Asians. Previous studies reviewed in Chapter 3 indicate that both Latino Americans and Asian Americans are heterogeneous populations comprised of individuals of different national backgrounds that differ considerably in terms of how recently they immigrated and in their educational attainment and success in the U.S. labor market.

We begin this chapter by presenting descriptive statistics for Latino and Asian students, disaggregated at the two-digit level of ethnicity, for educational outcomes and selected student characteristics. In the second section of this chapter we report the results of an analysis carried out at the two-digit level intended to shed additional light on the explanation of observed Latino-white and Asian-white differentials in community college outcomes. The third section takes a closer look at several of the disaggregated categories of Asian students for which our ability to explain observed Asian-white differentials in outcomes is modest. Our particular emphasis is on Vietnamese students. The final section sum-marizes the chapter.

DESCRIPTIVE STATISTICS AT THE TWO-DIGIT LEVEL OF ETHNICITY

To take advantage of the information contained in the two-digit ethnicity breakdown, we base our analysis on a restricted data set that omits, for both Latinos and Asians, observations that fall in the "other" and "undesignated" categories of race or ethnicity. This restriction re-duces the number of Latino students from 88,032 to 59,385 and the number of Asian students from 44,188 to 34,863. We combine male and female students for two reasons. The first is to preserve cell sizes for some of the small national origin categories such as South American within the one-digit Latino category and Cambodian and Laotian within the one-digit Asian category. The second reason is that our analysis at the one-digit level of race or ethnicity indicated only minor gender dif-ferences. In what follows, we measure gender by a dummy variable that takes the value 1 if the student is female, and 0 if male.

Beginning with Latinos, Table 6.1 displays outcome variables and selected explanatory variables for students whose national origin is Central America, Mexico, and South America. Mexican students are far more numerous than the other two categories of Latino students, and Mexicans appear much more likely to be U.S. citizens. Using the definition of first-generation immigrants specified in Chapter 5 (that is, students possessing a foreign high school degree and students who are not U.S. citizens and do not hold a foreign high school degree), only 27 percent of Mexicans are classified as immigrants compared to over 60 percent for Central Americans and South Americans. Disaggregating the "other" citizenship heading shown in the table, only Central American students are at all likely to be reported as refugees (3.7 percent), and only South Americans are at all likely to hold a student visa (2.4 percent).

Continuing to compare the attributes of Latino students, Mexicans are more likely than other Latino students to have earned a U.S. high school diploma. At the same time, receipt of either a U.S. or a foreign high school degree is very similar across all three categories—75.8

Table 6.1 Breakdown of Outcome Variables and Selected Explanatory Variables for Two-Digit Categories of Latinos, All Students

Variables	Central America	Mexico	South America
Outcomes[a]			
Transfer	0.083	0.083	0.109
AA degree	0.082	0.078	0.075
Total credits earned	26.5	24.9	25.0
Schooling			
U.S. high school diploma	0.622	0.684	0.512
Foreign high school diploma	0.136	0.051	0.209
No high school diploma	0.119	0.148	0.182
Took or needs ESL	0.131	0.106	0.303
Basic skills courses/all courses	0.219	0.191	0.270
Citizenship status			
U.S. citizen	0.427	0.742	0.426
Permanent resident	0.440	0.228	0.484
Other (all):	0.134	0.031	0.090
Temporary resident	0.044	0.012	0.023
Refugee	0.037	0.001	0.007
Student visa	0.002	0.000	0.024
Other or unknown	0.050	0.017	0.036
Other			
Credits attempted/semester	7.13	7.15	6.27
Transfer goal	0.277	0.301	0.282
GPA	2.07	2.01	2.22
Female	0.512	0.517	0.515
Number of students	8,094	48,444	2,847
First-generation immigrants (%)	60.3	27.1	62.3

[a] For comparison, white student means of the outcome variables are as follows: transfers, 15.6 percent; AA degree receipt, 10.0 percent; and total credits earned, 26.5 credits.

percent for Central Americans, 73.5 percent for Mexicans, and 72.1 percent for South Americans. As indicated by the ESL variable, South American students are considerably more likely than Mexicans and Central Americans to lack fluency in English. South Americans also take a somewhat higher ratio of basic skills courses and enroll in a smaller average number of courses per semester. Female students are somewhat more prevalent than males across all three Latino categories.

Despite these differences in citizenship status, a U.S. educational background, and English proficiency, we report only small differences in the community college outcome variables. The transfer rate of South Americans (10.9 percent) is slightly higher than that of the other two groups, but even this rate is considerably lower than the white rate of 15.6 percent.[1] There is no real difference between Central Americans, Mexicans, and South Americans in receipt of an AA degree or in number of total credits earned. Associate's degree rates for each of the three Latino categories are slightly lower than the white rate of 10.0 percent, while the range of total credits earned of between 24.9 credits for Mexicans and 26.5 credits for Central Americans is comparable to the white mean of 26.5 credits.

Turning to Asian students, Table 6.2 exhibits more substantial variation by national origin in both outcome variables and the explanatory variables shown. Beginning with the outcome variables, transfer rates range from highs of 40.0 percent for Chinese students and 34.6 percent for Indians to lows of 10.5 percent and 10.3 percent, respectively, for students with Cambodian and Laotian heritages. Only Cambodians and Laotians report a lower transfer rate than the white rate (15.6 percent). Associate's degree receipt is clustered in the 6–14 percent range across seven of the eight two-digit Asian categories identified. The exception is the much higher 30.4 percent rate observed for the Japanese. As just noted, AA degree receipt for whites is 10.0 percent. Japanese students also report the highest number of total credits earned at 44.4 credits followed closely by Chinese and Vietnamese students who earned 40.8 credits and 40.4 credits, respectively. At the low end are Cambodian, Laotian, and Korean students with average credits earned of 28–30 credits. But even these low-end totals for Asians exceed the average for whites, as noted, of 26.5 credits.

Among the selected explanatory variables displayed in Table 6.2, probably the biggest difference appears for citizenship status. Filipino students are by far the most likely to be U.S. citizens (69.3 percent), while Cambodians, Laotians, and the Vietnamese are least likely. Funkhouser and Trejo (1995) describe that the percentage of immigrants from Southeast Asia rose dramatically in the late 1970s and early 1980s following the fall of Saigon and the end of the Vietnam War. Many of the Southeast Asian students we observe would be expected to be children of immigrants of this era and thus U.S. citizens. Hence, it is interesting to note that roughly three-quarters of Cambodian, Laotian, and Vietnamese students attending CCCS campuses are immigrants themselves. Indeed, under the "other" citizenship heading we report that 7.6 percent and 10.8 percent of Laotian and Vietnamese students, respectively, entered the U.S. as refugees. Percentages of refugees calculated for the other Asian categories are very close to zero. One other finding worth noting is that fully 38.5 percent of Japanese students hold student visas. The next highest student-visa ratio of just 14.1 percent is reported for Koreans.

In terms of educational background, proportions of Asians who have earned a U.S. high school degree range from a high of 74.6 percent for Filipinos to a low of 47.7 percent for the Japanese. However, Japanese students have among the highest percentage of U.S. plus foreign high school diplomas at about 84 percent. This percentage reaches a maximum of 87.5 percent for Indians. At the other extreme, only 61.6 percent of Cambodians possess either a U.S. or foreign high school diploma. The comparable figure for whites is about 77.5 percent.

Continuing with the educational background variables, Japanese and Vietnamese students have the greatest deficiency in English skills, with 34 percent and 38 percent, respectively, indicating a need for ESL courses. However, the Japanese have a relatively low basic skills course ratio of 10 percent. Only Filipinos are lower still at 8.9 percent. Cambodians, Laotians, and the Vietnamese report basic skills course ratios in the 21 to 28 percent interval. With a large number of credits attempted per semester and a low age distribution (not shown), the picture that emerges is that a relatively large number of Japanese students are sent by their parents to a California community college to gain fluency in English, earn an AA degree, and possibly transfer to a four-year college. These students may or may not desire to stay in this country once their schooling is completed. In contrast, Asian students of other ethnic backgrounds who are not already citizens are more likely to be

Table 6.2 Breakdown of Outcome Variables and Selected Explanatory Variables for Two-Digit Categories of Asians, All Students

Variable	Cambodia	China	Philippines	India	Japan	Korea	Laos	Vietnam
Outcomes[a]								
Transfer	0.105	0.400	0.191	0.346	0.247	0.273	0.103	0.246
AA degree	0.087	0.134	0.114	0.116	0.304	0.059	0.075	0.140
Total credits earned	29.7	40.8	32.1	37.0	44.4	30.0	28.9	40.4
Schooling								
U.S. high school diploma	0.557	0.576	0.746	0.624	0.477	0.583	0.692	0.485
Foreign high school diploma	0.059	0.243	0.107	0.251	0.361	0.261	0.055	0.299
No high school diploma	0.286	0.072	0.051	0.053	0.027	0.060	0.157	0.119
Took or needs ESL	0.256	0.305	0.045	0.103	0.340	0.196	0.129	0.383
Basic skills ratio	0.282	0.120	0.089	0.102	0.100	0.141	0.225	0.207
Citizenship status								
U.S. citizen	0.222	0.477	0.693	0.427	0.455	0.386	0.308	0.267
Permanent resident	0.713	0.382	0.276	0.449	0.103	0.415	0.575	0.586
Other (all)	0.065	0.141	0.031	0.124	0.442	0.199	0.117	0.147
Temporary resident	0.009	0.002	0.004	0.009	0.006	0.006	0.008	0.007
Refugee	0.014	0.009	0.002	0.029	0.002	0.002	0.076	0.108
Student visa	0.006	0.094	0.003	0.028	0.385	0.141	0.010	0.005
Other or unknown	0.035	0.036	0.021	0.058	0.048	0.050	0.023	0.027

Other

Credits attempted/ semester	7.22	8.24	7.89	7.87	9.38	8.22	8.42	8.19
Transfer goal	0.319	0.427	0.428	0.398	0.428	0.443	0.386	0.419
GPA	2.09	2.59	2.15	2.41	2.66	2.32	2.05	2.45
Female	0.540	0.532	0.489	0.491	0.544	0.516	0.489	0.468
Number of students	774	9,360	9,760	1,519	2,555	3,193	708	6,994
First-generation immigrants (%)	78.6	57.3	35.0	61.2	55.5	65.6	70.8	76.6

[a] For comparison, white student means of the outcome variables are as follows: transfers, 15.6 percent; AA degree received, 10.0 percent; and total credits earned, 26.5 credits.

"true" immigrants in the sense that they are committed to working in the U.S. labor market following their schooling.

It is also interesting to compare the characteristics of the three largest Asian ethnic categories—namely, the Chinese, Filipinos, and Vietnamese. Filipino students appear to be the most advantaged in view of their high rates of U.S. citizenship and possession of a U.S. high school diploma coupled with their modest need for ESL training and low basic skills course ratio. On the other hand, Vietnamese students might be expected to be at a substantial disadvantage given their relatively recent immigration status, substantial need for ESL, and relatively high basic skills course ratio. In fact, Filipino students turn out to lag behind both Chinese and Vietnamese students on all three of our educational outcome measures. In a two-way comparison of Chinese and Vietnamese students, the Vietnamese have a substantially lower transfer rate than the Chinese. On the other hand, Vietnamese students report a slightly higher AA degree receipt rate, and average total credits completed are essentially the same as that for the Chinese.

RESULTS FOR OUTCOME VARIABLES DISAGGREGATING BY NATIONAL ORIGIN

Making use of the two-digit detail on national origin, Tables 6.3 and 6.4, respectively, assess the effects of holding constant our five categories of explanatory variables (and gender) on estimated Latino-white and Asian-white gaps in transfers, AA degree receipt, and total credits earned. Recall from Chapter 5 that at the individual student level we are able to control for four categories of explanatory variables: 1) background variables, including academic preparation and immigration status; 2) financial need; 3) educational goals; and 4) community college performance measures. The fifth category measured at the college level includes institutional and community characteristics.

We begin with Latino students in Table 6.3. As noted earlier, students of Mexican heritage are by far the most numerous category of Latino students, and the results in the second column closely echo those reported for all Latinos in Chapter 5 (see Table 5.8 on p. 86). For student transfers, that is, standardizing for student-level and college-level vari-

**Table 6.3 Comparison of Unadjusted and Regression-Adjusted Gaps
in Outcome Variables for Two-Digit Categories of Latinos,
All Students[a]**

Outcome	Central America-white	Mexico-white	South America-white
Transfer			
Unadjusted	−0.073	−0.073	−0.047
Adjusted	−0.015	−0.018**	0.016**
AA degree receipt			
Unadjusted	−0.018	−0.022	−0.025
Adjusted	0.014**	0.010**	0.017**
Total credits earned			
Unadjusted	0.0	−1.6	−1.5
Adjusted	3.2**	2.8**	4.1**

NOTE: **Statistically significant regression coefficient at the 0.05 level. $N = 254{,}512$.
[a] Regression-adjusted gaps control for differences in all five categories of explanatory variables.

ables reduces the observed Mexican-white gap of 7.3 percentage points to just 1.8 percentage points. Much the same result is obtained for the identical 7.3-percentage-point transfer gap between Central American and white students and for the smaller 4.7 percentage point gap for students of South American heritage. The small (or zero) observed gaps in Table 6.3 favoring whites in AA degrees and total credits earned leave little to be explained, and our regression-adjusted gap estimates actually reverse sign once adjustment has been made for differences in the explanatory variables.

For Asian students, Table 6.4 shows substantially more variation across national origin categories in sign and size of observed gaps and in the effects of standardizing. Beginning with transfer rates, Cambodians and Laotians are the two categories of Asian students that lag behind whites. For these students, standardizing reduces differences in means of about 5 percentage points to essentially zero for Cambodians and to 2.8 percentage points for Laotians. Standardizing also cuts in half the small positive gap (3.5 percentage points) observed for Filipinos. A larger positive gap of 9.1 percentage points is observed for Japanese students, and, again, standardizing essentially eliminates the gap. Applying the decomposition analysis used in Chapter 5 to the Japanese-white differ-

Table 6.4 Comparison of Unadjusted and Regression-Adjusted Gaps in Outcome Variables for Two-Digit Categories of Asians, All Students[a]

Variable category	Cambodia-white	China-white	Philippines-white	Indian-white	Japan-white	Korea-white	Laos-white	Vietnam-white
Transfer								
Unadjusted	-0.051	0.244	0.035	0.190	0.091	0.117	-0.053	0.090
Adjusted	-0.002	0.186**	0.019**	0.157**	0.018	0.088**	-0.028**	0.094**
AA receipt								
Unadjusted	-0.013	0.034	0.014	0.016	0.204	-0.041	-0.025	0.040
Adjusted	0.011	-0.007	0.011**	-0.005	0.129**	-0.057**	-0.018	0.027**
Total credits earned								
Unadjusted	3.2	14.3	5.6	10.5	17.9	3.5	2.4	13.9
Adjusted	5.5**	3.8**	3.0**	5.3**	2.4**	-3.3**	-0.4	6.9**

NOTE: **Statistically significant regression coefficient at the 0.05 level. $N = 254{,}512$.
[a] Regression-adjusted gaps control for differences in all five categories of explanatory variables.

ential indicates that the most important factor in explaining the higher transfer rate of Japanese students is our set of financial need measures, followed closely by the community college progress variables.

Table 6.4 also indicates that standardizing has less effect in diminishing the large gaps in transfer rates favoring Chinese, Indian, Korean, and Vietnamese students. The largest of these positive gaps is observed for the Chinese (24.4 percentage points). This gap falls only modestly to 18.6 percentage points (a 23.7 percent reduction) controlling for differences in the explanatory variables. Reductions in the observed gaps for students with an Indian or Korean heritage are also quite small—17.4 percent and 24.8 percent, respectively. For Vietnamese students, finally, the observed gap of 9.0 percentage points is essentially unaffected by standardization.

Moving to AA degree receipt, by far the largest of the positive gaps observed appears for the Japanese (20.4 percentage points), and we are successful in reducing this gap to 12.9 percentage points. Japanese students also report the largest positive gap in total credits earned of 17.9 credits. After standardizing, this gap falls to only 2.4 credits. Other large gaps in total credits earned are observed for the Chinese, Indians, and Vietnamese, and, similarly, each of these gaps is reduced substantially by standardization. After standardizing, the largest regression-adjusted gap still remaining appears for Vietnamese students at 6.9 credits.

Overall, Tables 6.3 and 6.4 indicate that we are less successful in explaining observed gaps in our outcome variables for Asian students than we are for Latino students. Among Asians, in addition, we seem to do less well for student transfers than for the other two outcome variables. Specifically, large regression-adjusted gaps in transfer rates remain for Chinese, Indian, and Korean students. But at least we had some success in reducing the very large observed gaps. For Vietnamese students, however, we had no success at all in reducing the observed 9.0-percentage-point gap.

In the next section, we examine three possible explanations for the substantial regression-adjusted gaps in educational outcomes that remain for Chinese, Indian, and Korean students, and especially for the Vietnamese.

ACCOUNTING FOR UNEXPLAINED GAPS FOR ASIANS

Differences in Family Income

In Chapter 5, we described 2000 census data for California showing that Asians on average enjoy a slightly higher median family income than whites, and that the median family income of whites substantially exceeds that of Latinos. We noted that since family background measures are not available in FTF data, we included among our college-level explanatory variables measures of community median family income and average education. But since these community variables are imprecise measures of the economic circumstances of particular families, it is quite possible that our Asian variable may reflect the relatively high incomes of Asian families.

Continuing to use 2000 census data for California, Table 6.5 presents median family income estimates for Latino and Asian families broken down at the two-digit level of ethnicity. The table shows that both Central American and Mexican families earn considerably less than South Americans. But even larger variation appears for Asian families. At the top end of the family income distribution are Indian and Japanese families, with annual earnings of about $77,000 and $74,000, respectively. Chinese families follow with average earnings in excess of $66,000. At the low end for Asians, Cambodian and Laotian families earn less than $30,000 annually.

We noted in Chapter 5 that differentials in family income between Asians, whites, and Latinos are likely to overstate differentials we would observe for families of community college students. The reason is that high-income Asian families are more likely to send their children to a UC or CSU campus as opposed to a community college. Nevertheless, with the very high average family incomes shown in Table 6.5, the possibility that ethnicity variables capture unmeasured family background variables seems especially applicable to Indian and Chinese students. This omitted-variable explanation has less power, however, in the context of Vietnamese and Korean students for whom average family incomes are well below the all-Asian average, which is close to the average for white families.

Table 6.5 Median Family Income for Latinos and Asians Residing in California, by Two-Digit Ethnic Categories, 1996[a]

	Median family income ($)
Latinos	
Central America	32,128
Mexico	35,772
South America	50,149
All Latinos	35,980
Asians	
Cambodia	26,183
China	66,467
Philippines	65,899
India	77,110
Japan	73,884
Korea	48,536
Laos	29,755
Vietnam	49,114
All Asians	61,383

[a] For reference, median family income for white families is $60,216 and for black families, $39,726.
SOURCE: U.S. Census (2000).

Differences in Refugee Status

In view of the high percentage of immigrants among Vietnamese students (see Table 6.2), a second explanation worth exploring is based on Borjas's (1982) distinction between *political refugees* and *economic immigrants*. As briefly described in Chapter 3, the primary difference between the two immigrant groups is in the probability of return migration. Political refugees have little chance of returning to their home countries, and consequently they have a strong incentive to adapt rapidly to the U.S. labor market. On the other hand, economic immigrants can more easily return to the country of origin, thereby reducing their incentive to invest in U.S.-specific capital. Using data for Latino immigrants who differ by ethnicity, Borjas uses Cubans as an example of political refugees who face a high cost of returning home, and Mexicans and Puerto Ricans as examples of economic immigrants whose cost is much lower. Consistent with his hypothesis, Cuban immigrants are found to invest more in U.S. schooling and enjoy faster growth in earnings than any other of the groups of Latino immigrants studied.

Additional evidence on the political refugee/economic immigrant distinction is reported in a recent paper by Cortes (2004) that considers Asian as well as Latino immigrants. In her analysis, political refugees come from eight countries, including Cambodia, Laos, and Vietnam. Political refugees from these countries are compared to economic immigrants specified as immigrants from 14 countries or regions, including Mexico, Central America, the Caribbean, South America, and the Philippines. Her findings are strongly consistent with Borjas's hypothesis. Examining immigrants who arrived in the United States between 1975 and 1980, Cortes finds little initial difference in 1980 between the two groups in English language skills and probability of U.S. citizenship, but lower earnings for political refugees. At the same time, political refugees are much more likely to be enrolled in the U.S. educational system. Ten years later in 1990, political refugees are found to have enjoyed greater earnings growth than economic immigrants. They also have surpassed economic immigrants in English-language skills, are more likely to be citizens, and continue to have a higher school enrollment rate.[2]

In discussing Table 6.2, we noted that, with the exception of Laotians, the proportion of refugees among Vietnamese students of nearly 11 percent is much higher than for any other Asian ethic group. The political refugee status of many Vietnamese students, and for others the refugee status of their parents, is thus likely to be important in understanding the high transfer rate shown in our data for the Vietnamese. Although they are not as likely to be political refugees as the Vietnamese, Chinese Americans also face restrictions on traveling to and from their home country, potentially making the Borjas hypothesis helpful in explaining the high transfer rate of Chinese students. More broadly, the high cost of return migration for Asian immigrants in general may be part of what is termed the "Asian culture." As mentioned in Chapter 3, what is usually meant by Asian culture is a strongly held belief by Asian families that education is the primary mechanism for getting ahead in American society. Hence, Asian children are encouraged to do well in school, and their parents exhibit a willingness to make substantial financial sacrifices to make sure that their children are able to pursue their schooling on a full-time basis.

Conversely, the low-cost option of return migration for many Mexicans and other Latinos may be useful in understanding the low transfer rate shown in our data for Latino students and, more broadly, in understanding what was termed in Chapter 3 "Hispanic culture." Hispanic culture essentially is the attitude within the community that the primary role of family members is to enhance the economic well-being of the family, whether the family is centered in the United States or in the home country. Because of this attitude, Latino community college students may exhibit a stronger interest than others in occupational skills training, while being more constrained in terms of the hours they can commit to their schooling.

The Effect of Geographic Clustering

A third explanation of unexplained gaps in educational outcomes emphasizes the geographic clustering of immigrant groups in ethnic enclaves. In Chapter 5, we examined the relationship across community colleges between the concentration or "clustering" of students of a particular ethnic background and their ethnicity-specific transfer rate. In this analysis, college transfer rates were adjusted for differences in student-level explanatory variables. Our results showed an important difference between Latinos and Asians. While a greater clustering of Latino students is found to have a negative effect on the standardized transfer rate of Latinos, the share of Asians increases the Asian standardized transfer rate. We interpreted this finding in the context of Borjas's (1999) suggestion that the geographic clustering of immigrant groups in ethnic enclaves may have important labor market effects—effects that may be either positive or negative.

Even among Asian immigrants, the Vietnamese appear to be especially concentrated in particular geographic areas. In his useful study of the rapid assimilation of Vietnamese immigrants, Rose (1985) remarks on the high concentrations of Vietnamese families in California and specifically in Orange County and the city of San Jose in Santa Clara County. Zhou and Bankston (1998, Chapter 2) add the information that despite an official U.S. policy of geographic dispersion for Vietnamese immigrants, internal migration within the United States has resulted in a net increase of Vietnamese families in California, especially in the metropolitan areas of Orange County, Los Angeles, San Diego, and San

Jose. In fact, Vietnamese communities in the Orange County cities of Garden Grove and Westminster are known as "Little Saigon" because of the concentration of Vietnamese families in an area that a couple of decades earlier was almost exclusively white.

More information on the geographic concentration of immigrant groups in California appears in California Department of Finance (no date), which supplies information, by county, on the nationality of immigrants admitted as legal permanent residents in 2000. Table 6.6 lists the top five counties of residence for immigrants from the four countries that supplied the largest number of immigrants. For Vietnamese immigrants, Orange and Santa Clara Counties are numbers one and two on this list. Note that over 50 percent of Vietnamese immigrants settled in these two counties. In contrast, Los Angles County is by far the most common county of residence for the other immigrant groups shown.[3] Since they are *community* colleges, a high concentration of members of a particular ethnic group in a community is likely to mean a high concentration of students with the same ethnic background in the local community college or colleges.

To follow up on the hypothesis that their academic success is at least partially due to clustering, we investigate the distribution of Vietnamese FTF students across the 79 CCCS colleges that report ethnicity at the two-digit level. Vietnamese students do indeed appear to be highly concentrated in a small number of community colleges in Orange and Santa Clara Counties. Of the 6,994 Vietnamese students in our FTF data set, 2,297 students, or 32.8 percent, are enrolled in just five community colleges in two of the four Orange County community college (CC) districts. The colleges are Coastline, Golden West, and Orange Coast in the Coast CC district, and Cypress and Fullerton in the North Orange County CC district. For colleges in the Coast CC district, Vietnamese students as a proportion of all FTF are about 28 percent for both Coastline College and Golden West College and about 13 percent for Orange Coast College. Vietnamese student enrollment is about 9 percent for Cyprus College and 5 percent for Fullerton College in the North Orange County CC District. These colleges are all within close commuting distance to the cities of Garden Grove and Westminster—the communities identified earlier as "Little Saigon." It is also interesting to note that the number of Vietnamese students served by the three colleges in the other two Orange County districts (South Orange

**Table 6.6 Top Five Counties of Residence of Legal Immigrants in 2000
Who Chose to Live in California, by Selected Countries of Birth**

Country	Percent
Mexico	
Los Angeles	29.5
Orange	10.8
San Diego	9.1
Riverside	5.4
San Bernadino	4.5
Other counties	40.7
China	
Los Angeles	30.8
San Francisco	21.0
Santa Clara	12.8
Alameda	12.8
San Mateo	4.1
Other counties	18.5
Philippines	
Los Angeles	32.4
San Diego	11.9
Santa Clara	9.4
Alameda	7.2
Orange	6.3
Other counties	32.8
Vietnam	
Orange	28.7
Santa Clara	23.7
Los Angeles	21.5
San Diego	5.9
Alameda	5.3
Other counties	14.9

SOURCE: California Department of Finance (n.d.).

County CC District and Rancho Santiago CC District) is much smaller, indicating that even in Orange County, Vietnamese students are highly concentrated geographically.

The two community colleges serving the city of San Jose (Evergreen Valley College and San Jose City College) in the San Jose-Evergreen CC district are not included among the 79 colleges that report ethnic origin at the two-digit level.[4] Nevertheless, there is a heavy concentration of Vietnamese students in DeAnza College and Mission College serving the nearby Santa Clara County communities of Cupertino and Santa Clara, respectively.[5] Together, these two colleges enroll 973 Vietnamese, or about 14 percent of all Vietnamese students. About 10 percent of all FTF enrolled in DeAnza College are Vietnamese, and the same proportion for Mission College is about 25 percent. Taken together, it is striking that just seven community colleges located in Orange County and Santa Clara County enroll nearly half of all Vietnamese students included in our data set.

Potentially important in understanding the impact of the clustering of Vietnamese students is a concept termed "ethnic capital" in the labor economics literature. As described by Borjas (1995), ethnic capital is the idea that the economic success of today's workers depends not only on parental skills, but also on the average skills of the ethnic group in the parents' generation. The empirical evidence he presents indicates, for persons raised in segregated neighborhoods, that ethnicity remains a significant explanatory variable even after controlling for the effects of family background and neighborhood.

Focusing on the Vietnamese, sociologists Zhou and Bankston (1998, Chapter 6) describe in detail a similar concept that they term *social capital*. The authors observe that in Vietnamese neighborhoods, even those that are low income, families are connected to one another through the community in a way that reinforces the efforts of parents and acts as a bridge to mainstream society. To test for the importance of social capital, Zhou and Bankston use 1990 census data to examine the impact of race or ethnicity on the probability of dropping out of high school. As expected, Vietnamese (along with Chinese) students have a much lower probability of dropping out than whites or blacks, even after controlling for such student characteristics as age and English proficiency and such family background variables as father's education and family poverty status. However, the estimated Vietnamese effect basically disappears when a Vietnamese residential concentration variables is added to the analysis. In other words, the likelihood of becoming a high school dropout decreases significantly for Vietnamese students as the probability of living around other Vietnamese increases.

SUMMARY

This chapter continued the analysis begun in Chapter 5 that explained observed gaps in community college outcome variables favoring whites over Latinos and Asians over whites. These outcome variables include student transfers, receipt of an AA degree, and total credits earned. In this chapter we are able to expand our analysis by exploiting a more detailed breakdown by ethnicity for Latinos and Asians.

Our earlier analysis demonstrated that we can explain reasonably well the observed Latino-white gaps with our four categories of student-level explanatory variables and college-specific variables. Breaking down Latinos by ethnic background, this finding is echoed in results reported in this chapter for Central Americans and South Americans, as well as for the numerically far larger group of Mexicans. It is worth noting that Central American and South American students are more likely to be immigrants than are Mexican students.

Our ability to explain Asian-white gaps in educational outcomes in Chapter 5 was mixed. Results presented in this chapter help to clarify this analysis. Disaggregating Asians by ethnicity, we are able to substantially explain observed negative gaps in transfers and AA degrees for Cambodians and Laotians, and observed positive gaps in all three outcome variables for Filipinos and the Japanese. We are less successful in explaining positive, and typically larger, observed gaps in student transfers for the Chinese, Indians, and Koreans. We are not successful at all in explaining the large observed gap in transfers for the Vietnamese. The Chinese, Filipinos, and Vietnamese are numerically the largest categories of Asian students enrolled in CCCS campuses.

To understand these unexplained gaps in outcome variables for Chinese, Indian, Korean, and Vietnamese students, we considered three possible explanations discussed in the labor economics and sociology literatures. These explanations emphasize 1) unobserved differences in family background, including family income; 2) the political refugee/ economic immigrant distinction; and 3) geographic clustering in ethnic enclaves.

Focusing our attention on the three largest groups of Asian students, unobserved differences in family income appear to be a relevant consideration for Indian and Chinese students given the very high average family incomes of Indian and Chinese families in California. But this explanation is less persuasive for the Vietnamese for whom average family income is much lower. The second explanation stresses the special incentives for political refugees to invest in U.S.-specific human capital. This is likely to be more important for Vietnamese students since more than three-quarters are first-generation immigrants. Moreover, refugees represent a large proportion of Vietnamese students who are immigrants. The third explanation centers on the development of valuable ethnic capital in ethnically segregated communities. We provide evidence that this explanation is potentially important for the Vietnamese population in California because of its concentration in a small number of metropolitan areas and the clustering of Vietnamese students in a handful of community colleges.

Notes

1. The overall white transfer rate of 15.6 percent is the weighted average of the white female rate of 16.3 percent and the white male rate of 14.9 percent reported in Table 5.2 in the previous chapter. Similarly, for whites, the overall AA degree receipt rate is 10.0 percent and average credits earned is 26.5 credits.
2. Writing in the sociology literature, Rose (1985) also argues that the key to understanding the rapid assimilation of Vietnamese immigrants is their political refugee status. That is, rather than being pulled away by the attraction of a better life in America, the Vietnamese were driven out by the fear of suffering persecution in their homeland. The prevailing view that the Vietnamese were "war victims" rather than competitors for scarce jobs led, according to Rose, to a much broader acceptance in the United States than otherwise would have been expected. The federal government, working with private voluntary agencies, provided important funding and logistical support. But even with this relief from the financial burden, Rose suggests that the willingness of thousands of Americans to serve as sponsors and to provide other forms of assistance to Indochinese refugees was directly related to a moral obligation to help these victims of the war.
3. Broadly speaking, Orange and Santa Clara Counties can be characterized as suburban, whereas L.A. County is urban. As discussed in Chapter 7, the literature

suggests that community colleges located in suburban areas are more likely to be responsive to local labor market conditions than are colleges located in either urban or rural areas.

4. Evergreen Valley College and San Jose City College are, however, heavily Asian. Measured at the one-digit level, both colleges report that 45 percent of their first-time freshmen are Asians.

5. Recall from Chapter 3 that public high schools in the cities of Cupertino and San Jose are used by Hwang (2005) to illustrate the pressure for higher academic standards exerted in communities with growing proportions of Asian families.

7
Community Colleges' Responsiveness to Local Labor Market Demand

The second of the two research issues outlined in Chapter 1 is to evaluate the success of community colleges in meeting the skill requirements of local employers. In Chapter 4, we described three approaches taken in the literature to investigate this issue. We concluded that chapter with a discussion of a new approach that examines the match, at the local labor market level, between occupational training supplied by community colleges and employers' demand for skills. We implement that new approach in this chapter.

We begin this chapter by considering two levels of the CCCS administrative structure at which we might measure labor market responsiveness. These are the individual community college (CC) and the community college district. The next two sections concern the supply of occupational skills by colleges and the demand for these skills by local employers. On the supply side, we describe our use of information from the 1996 FTF cohort on the flow of new credits completed over the 1996–2002 period. Credits completed are classified by the Taxonomy of Programs (TOP) classification system. TOP code information is used to construct for each college the occupational distribution of skills supplied. The demand side uses occupational labor demand projection provided online by the Labor Market Information Division (LMID) of California's Employment Development Department. These occupational labor demand projections, which are also classified by TOP codes, are available at the county level.

We then bring labor supply and demand together to assess the quality of matches between skills supplied by community colleges and local employers' demand for trained workers. Match quality is examined at the level of the individual community college and at the CC district level. The final section summarizes the chapter.

131

APPROACHES TO MATCHING WITHIN THE CCCS

Table 7.1 lists the 31 California counties that are served by one or more community colleges and for which LMID labor demand projections are available. These include large, heavily populated counties such as Los Angeles County with an estimated 2003 population of 9.9 million persons. As seen in the table, L.A. County is served by 21 community colleges organized into 13 community college districts, which include the nine-campus Los Angeles CC district. At the other extreme, rural counties such as Humboldt County on the northern California Pacific Coast are also served by a community college (College of the Redwoods) in a single campus CC district. The estimated 2003 population of Humboldt County is only about 128,000 persons.

In addition to the 31 counties, LMID labor demand projections are available for four labor market consortia, each of which contains several lightly populated counties. The purpose of each consortium is to coordinate employment and training services for economically disadvantaged and dislocated workers residing in member counties. As described in Table 7.1, the Northern Rural Training and Employment Consortium (NorTEC) is served by three community colleges, the Golden Sierra Consortium is served by two colleges, and the Mother Lode and North Central Consortia are each served by a single college. Number of counties included in consortia range from 4 in the Mother Lode Consortium to 7 in NorTEC. Taking into account the 21 counties included in consortia, just 6 of California's 58 counties do not have a community college located in the county or are not part of a consortium served by one or more community colleges.

Table 7.1 also lists the 106 community colleges that we include in our analysis.[1] These colleges are organized into 71 community college districts. Most rural communities are served by a single community college that comprises its own district. In urban areas, districts may also be single-campus districts, but often they consist of more than one campus. Moreover, larger urban areas are typically served by more than one district. As already noted, L.A. County is served by 13 districts—12 single-campus districts and the very large multicampus Los Angeles CC district.

Table 7.1 Breakdown of California Counties (and Consortia), Community College Districts, and Community Colleges

County/consortium[a]	Community college district	Community college[b]
Alameda	Chabot–Las Positas	Chabot and Las Positas
	Ohlone	Ohlone
	Peralta	Alameda, Laney, Merritt, and Vista
Butte	Butte-Glenn	Butte
Contra Costa	Contra Costa	Contra Costa, Diablo Valley, and Los Medanos
Fresno	State Center	Fresno City and Reedly
	West Hills	West Hills
Golden Sierra Consortium (Alpine, El Dorado, Nevada, Placer, Sierra)	Lake Tahoe	Lake Tahoe
	Sierra Joint	Sierra
Humboldt	Redwoods	Redwoods
Imperial	Imperial	Imperial Valley
Kern	Kern	Bakersfield, Cerro Coso, and Porterville[c]
	West Kern	Taft
Los Angeles	Antelope Valley	Antelope Valley
	Cerritos	Cerritos
	Citrus	Citrus
	Compton	Compton
	El Camino	El Camino
	Glendale	Glendale
	Long Beach	Long Beach City
	Los Angeles	East L.A., L.A. City, L.A. Harbor, L.A. Mission, L.A. Pierce, L.A. Southwest, L.A. Trade-Tech, L.A. Valley, and West L.A.
	Mt. San Antonio	Mt. San Antonio
	Pasadena Area	Pasadena City
	Rio Hondo	Rio Hondo
	Santa Clarita	Canyons
	Santa Monica	Santa Monica City
Marin	Marin	Marin
Mendocino	Mendocino-Lake	Mendocino
Merced	Merced	Merced

(continued)

Table 7.1 (continued)

County/consortium[a]	Community college district	Community college[b]
Monterey	Hartnell	Hartnell
	Monterey Peninsula	Monterey Peninsula
Mother Lode Consortium (Amador, Calaveras, Mariposa, and Tuolumne)	Yosemite[d]	Columbia
Napa	Napa Valley	Napa Valley
North Central Consortium (Colusa, Glenn, Lake, Sutter, and Yuba)	Yuba	Yuba
Northern Rural Training and Employment Consortium (Del Norte, Lassen, Modoc, Plumas, Siskiyou, Tehama, and Trinity)	Lassen Feather River Siskiyou Joint	Lassen Feather River Siskiyous
Orange	Coast	Coastline, Golden West, and Orange Coast
	North Orange County	Cypress and Fullerton
	Rancho Santiago	Santa Ana[e]
	South Orange County	Irvine Valley and Saddleback
Riverside	Desert	Desert
	Mt. San Jacinto	Mt. San Jacinto
	Palo Verde	Palo Verde
	Riverside	Riverside
Sacramento	Los Rios	American River, Consumnes River, and Sacramento City
San Bernadino	Barstow	Barstow
	Chaffey	Chaffey
	San Bernardino	Crafton Hills and San Bernardino Valley
	Victor Valley	Victor Valley
San Diego	Grossmont-Cuyamaca	Cuyamaca and Grossmont
	MiraCosta	MiraCosta
	Palomar	Palomar
	San Diego	San Diego City, San Diego Mesa, and San Diego Miramar
	Southwestern	Southwestern

Table 7.1 (continued)

County/consortium[a]	Community college district	Community college[b]
San Francisco	San Francisco	San Francisco City
San Joaquin	San Joaquin Delta	San Joaquin Delta
San Luis Obispo	San Luis Obispo County	Cuesta
San Mateo	San Mateo County	Canada, San Mateo, and Skyline
Santa Barbara	Allan Hancock	Allan Hancock
	Santa Barbara	Santa Barbara City
Santa Clara	Foothill-DeAnza	DeAnza and Foothill
	Gavilan Joint	Gavilan
	San Jose–Evergreen	Evergreen Valley and San Jose City
	West Valley–Mission	Mission and West Valley
Santa Cruz	Cabrillo	Cabrillo
Shasta	Shasta-Tehama-Trinity	Shasta
Solano	Solano County	Solano
Sonoma	Sonoma County	Santa Rosa
Stanislaus	Yosemite[d]	Modesto
Tulare	Sequoias	Sequoias
Ventura	Ventura County	Moorpark, Oxnard, and Ventura

[a] Counties included in consortia are listed in parentheses.

[b] Santiago Canyon College in Orange County and Copper Mountain College in San Bernadino are not listed. See the explanation in Note 1.

[c] As indicated, Porterville College is part of the Kern CC district; however, it is located in Tulare County rather than Kern County. In the subsequent analysis, Tulare County is counted as a multicollege county.

[d] Yosemite CC district appears twice in this column because it includes two colleges (Columbia College and Modesto College) located in two different counties. Columbia College is in Tuolumne County, and Modesto College is in Stanislaus County.

[e] Santiago Canyon College, along with Santa Ana College, is part of the Rancho Santiago CC district. Consequently, we treat the Rancho Santiago CC district as a multicampus district, even though Santiago Canyon College is excluded from our analysis.

Local labor markets are commonly defined by the geographical area within which workers can commute to jobs by car. In California, we suggest that this definition is reasonably satisfied by the county. Table 7.1 indicates the two levels of community college administration at which we might consider matching the supply of trained workers with county-level occupational demand projections.

1. Matching by college. This approach takes all 106 individual colleges as the unit of observation. That is, we examine the match between the supply of trained workers for each college and employment projections for the county in which the college is located, even if more than one college supplies trained workers to the local labor market. The implicit assumption involved in this approach is that each college, if it is to be viewed as market responsive, provides training in all occupational fields of study in which job opportunities are available in its county.

2. Matching by district. This approach assumes that the proper level for evaluating labor market responsiveness is the district rather than the individual college. The underlying assumption is that community colleges located in multicampus districts may choose to specialize in the training they provide. For example, consider a county that is experiencing growth in engineering technology and health care jobs. (These are two of the occupational fields of study appearing in Table 7.2 and following tables.) If the county is served by a district consisting of two colleges, College A may choose to emphasize an engineering technology curriculum and deemphasize training in health care. At the same time, College B may choose to emphasize health care programs and deemphasize engineering technology. In Gill and Leigh (2004), we define as *specialization* the choice by a community college to emphasize one curriculum area while deemphasizing another. While neither college appears by itself to be responsive to labor market demand in this example, their individual efforts at specializing complement each other with the end result that their district is labor market responsive.

Implementing Approach 2 for multicampus districts requires matching the supply of trained workers aggregated across the colleges in a district to employment projections for the county in which the district is located. There are 71 observations taking this approach.

VARIATION IN THE SUPPLY OF SKILLS

First-time-freshmen student records include information on all courses taken over a six-year period. Each course is distinguished by number of credits attempted and completed, and by field of study measured at the four-digit and occasionally even the five-digit level using the TOP classification system. Between credits attempted and completed, we use information on credits completed since our aim is to measure the supply of trained workers to the local labor market. There are two possible concerns about using credits completed to measure the supply of skills. First, noncredit courses are not measured in FTF data. To the extent that the customized training courses described in Chapter 4 are noncredit courses, credits completed may understate the true supply of skills furnished by a community college. Second, it might be argued that a preferred training measure is programs or certificates, rather than credits, completed. As indicated in Chapter 5, however, relatively few community college students complete AA degrees, and even fewer complete certificates. Moreover, in a study referred to in Chapter 4, Kane and Rouse (1995) demonstrate that credits completed are strongly related to subsequent labor market earnings.

Fields of study in FTF data are distinguished by well over 300 occupational TOP codes. To get a feel for the level of detail included in this classification system, take as an example the two-digit category Engineering Technology (09). Within this broad occupational category, an example of an occupational program distinguished at the four-digit level is Aeronautical and Aviation Technology (0950); and, within this four-digit category, an example of an occupational program at the five-digit level is Aviation Power Plant Mechanic (09502). In addition to the detail available for field of study, the CCCS Chancellor's Office singles out TOP codes considered vocational. All 64 of the four- and five-digit categories included under Engineering Technology are classified as vocational. In other two-digit categories such as Foreign Languages (11), none of the included 17 four- and five-digit categories are vocational.

As shown in Table 7.2, we use this information on credits completed classified by TOP codes to develop two supply-side measures: 1) vocational credits completed by cohort members over a six-year period measured as a proportion of all credits completed during this period, and 2) the occupational distribution of vocational credits completed. Specifically, our 12-category classification scheme is the following (TOP codes are indicated in parentheses):

- Agriculture technology and sciences (01)
- Business (05)
- Communications (06)
- Information technology (07)
- Engineering technology, including architectural and oceanic technology (02, 09 except 0952, and 1920)
- Construction crafts (0952)
- Commercial arts (10)
- Health care, including biomedical technology (12 and 0430)
- Fashion and child development (1302–1305 and 1399)
- Food and hospitality (1306–1307)
- Commercial services (30)
- Other services, including education and community services (08, 1402, 1602, 21, and 4931).

With a few exceptions, these 12 categories follow a two-digit TOP code breakdown.[2]

To illustrate our supply-side measures, we report in Table 7.2 descriptive statistics for Santa Barbara City College, Santa Monica City College, and Los Angeles Trade-Tech College. Santa Barbara City College and Santa Monica City College are selected as representative colleges that emphasize a traditional academic curriculum leading to transfer to four-year colleges and universities (see Gill and Leigh 2004). On the other hand, L.A. Trade-Tech markets itself as the primary campus within the Los Angeles CC District for acquiring occupational skills saleable in the local labor market. Santa Monica City College and L.A. Trade-Tech are in different community college districts but the same county (Los Angeles County). Santa Monica City College is the only campus in the Santa Monica CC district, while L.A. Trade-Tech is part of the nine-campus Los Angeles CC district. Santa Barbara City College, located in Santa Barbara County, is the only campus in the Santa Barbara CC district.

Table 7.2 Supply-Side Variables for Representative Community Colleges, 1996 FTF Data

Variable	Santa Barbara City College	Santa Monica College	L.A. Trade-Tech
Voc-ed credits/all credits	0.20	0.19	0.55
Occupational distribution of voc-ed credits (%)			
Agriculture technology	3.3	—	—
Business	22.7	31.1	12.6
Communications	3.0	4.1	1.5
Information technology	14.5	18.5	5.9
Engineering technology	13.8	7.6	23.8
Construction crafts	—	—	16.2
Commercial arts	3.3	11.0	3.3
Health care	9.6	2.6	4.9
Fashion and child development	4.6	8.2	17.9
Food and hospitality	11.3	3.1	6.3
Commercial services	3.5	7.0	6.8
Other services	10.5	6.7	0.7
Average number of credits completed	26.6	22.8	16.6

NOTE: A dash (—) indicates that the college does not have a presence providing training in the particular occupation.

A natural approach to developing our supply-side measures would be, for each college, to aggregate across FTF students enrolled to arrive at total credits completed in all programs, in vocational programs, and in each of our 12 occupational categories. College initially attended would seem to be a logical way to identify students' college affiliation. Indeed, as described in Chapter 5, we use college initially attended to append institution variables to the variables we obtain from student records. For the purpose of accurately describing a college's supply of occupational skills, the problem with this approach is the implicit assumption that students do not transfer between community colleges and that they do not simultaneously take courses at different colleges. But students do transfer and especially those residing in large metropolitan areas have the opportunity to enroll in different colleges in the same semester. Consequently, we construct our supply-side measures using an alternative approach that involves the following four-step protocol:

1.   Identify all students who completed at least one course at a college, say, Santa Barbara City College.

2.   Aggregate over these students to calculate the total number of credits completed at Santa Barbara City College.

3.   Of total credits completed at Santa Barbara City College, find the total number of vocational credits completed and calculate the proportion of vocational credits to all credits.

4.   Of all vocational credits completed at Santa Barbara City College, find the number of credits completed in each field-of-study category and calculate the percentage distribution of vocational credits.

The first row of Table 7.2 displays a striking difference in proportion of vocational credits completed between Santa Barbara City College and Santa Monica City College, on the one hand, and L.A. Trade-Tech, on the other. Only about one-fifth of all credits completed in the first two colleges are in vocational fields of study, whereas 55 percent of credits supplied by L.A. Trade-Tech are vocational. This difference is consistent with our a priori expectations regarding the transfer orientation of Santa Barbara City College and Santa Monica City College and the vocational orientation of L.A. Trade-Tech.

Sizable differences between colleges also appear in the occupational distributions of credits completed. Compared to Santa Barbara City College and Santa Monica City College, L.A. Trade-Tech supplies proportionately more credits in engineering technology, construction crafts (indeed, Santa Barbara City College and Santa Monica City College have no presence at all in this occupation), and fashion and child development. On the other hand, L.A. Trade-Tech students complete proportionately fewer credits in business, information technology, and, to a lesser extent, other services. The occupational distributions of credits are more alike for Santa Barbara City College and Santa Monica City College, although some noticeable differences still exist. In particular, Santa Monica City College supplies proportionately more credits in business and in commercial arts, while Santa Barbara City College has a larger presence in engineering technology, health care, and food and hospitality.

The final row of Table 7.2 shows the average number of total credits completed for any student who completed at least one credit at, say, Santa Barbara City College. On average, total credits completed are clearly much higher at the two transfer-oriented colleges than at L.A. Trade-Tech—60 percent higher for Santa Barbara City College and 37 percent higher for Santa Monica City College. As a point of reference, the data presented in Chapter 5 suggest that semester-equivalent credits completed measured across students attending all 108 CCCS colleges averages out to be 24.7 credits for males and 28.3 credits for females.[3] Note that these averages include credits taken at any CCCS campus, which allows for the possibilities of students transferring between community colleges or taking courses at two or more colleges simultaneously. Thus, the fact that the average number of credits completed at the three colleges are reasonably close to the average number of credits taken across all CCCS campuses indicates that most students who completed any credits at these colleges completed most of their credits at the same institution.

Using information for all 106 CCCS colleges, Table 7.3 describes variation in the supply of occupational training comparing colleges in single-campus districts to colleges in multicampus districts. The opportunity for specialization suggests, other things equal, that greater variation in our supply-side variables will be observed for colleges in multicampus districts than for those in single-campus districts. On the other hand, colleges in single-campus districts serve rural areas as well as large metropolitan areas, whereas colleges in multicampus districts predominately serve metropolitan areas. If the service areas of single-campus districts spanning both rural and metropolitan areas are more industrially diverse than service areas of multicampus districts (because of an emphasis on agriculture in rural areas, for example), greater supply-side variation may appear for colleges in single-campus districts.

A comparison of the means displayed in Table 7.3 shows only small differences between colleges in single-campus and multicampus districts. The mean proportion of voc-ed credits completed to all credits completed is very similar at 29.5 percent for colleges in single-campus districts and 26.3 percent for colleges in multicampus districts. For fields of study, the most common areas of training for both categories of colleges are business and other services. Training in business is somewhat more common for colleges in multicampus districts, while

Table 7.3 Measures of Variation in the Supply of Occupational Training Provided by Community Colleges, by CC District Affiliation (%)

Supply-side variable	Colleges in single-campus districts (N = 51)				Colleges in multicampus districts[a] (N = 55)			
	Mean	Minimum	Maximum	Inter-quartile range	Mean	Minimum	Maximum	Inter-quartile range
Voc-ed credits/all credits	29.5	19.5	56.3	5.7	26.3	16.4	54.7	7.8
Occupational distribution of credits								
Agriculture technology	3.5	0.0	31.2	5.4	1.8	0.0	17.6	2.0
Business	20.0	9.2	35.9	8.6	22.6	8.4	48.5	9.4
Communications	2.1	0.0	11.5	3.2	2.7	0.0	12.9	3.3
Information technology	12.4	2.2	28.0	9.7	14.7	3.6	43.7	6.9
Engineering technology	11.6	0.0	24.3	7.2	13.8	0.0	40.0	11.4
Construction crafts	1.1	0.0	11.6	1.6	1.5	0.0	16.1	1.5
Commercial arts	2.2	0.0	11.0	3.6	2.6	0.0	14.9	3.8
Health care	9.3	2.6	23.3	5.2	8.0	0.0	27.0	7.4
Fashion and child development	9.7	1.2	25.9	5.1	11.3	0.0	33.2	7.8
Food and hospitality	2.5	0.0	11.3	3.5	2.8	0.0	16.4	4.5
Commercial services	2.9	0.0	21.7	3.8	3.0	0.0	18.2	4.8
Other services	22.7	4.2	63.7	14.0	15.2	0.0	59.0	16.7

[a] Includes the Rancho Santiago CC district, of which Santa Ana College and Santiago Canyon College are members. As explained in Note 1, Santiago Canyon College is not included in our data.

training in other services is more common for colleges in single-campus districts. These two fields of study are followed in popularity on the supply side by information technology, engineering technology, and fashion and child development.

For both categories of district affiliation, we also report in Table 7.3 the minimum and maximum values of supply-side variables (indicating the range) and the inter-quartile (IQ) range. Large extreme values are shown for particular colleges in both district affiliation categories. Among colleges in single-campus districts, the maximum value of the voc-ed credits ratio is found for Palo Verde College (56.3 percent). This contrasts with a minimum value of only 19.5 percent for Santa Monica City College. For multicampus districts, minimum and maximum values appear for San Diego Mesa College (16.4 percent) and L.A. Trade-Tech (54.7 percent), respectively. Recall that earlier in this section we used Santa Monica City College (along with Santa Barbara City College) as an example of a college that emphasizes a traditional academic curriculum, while L.A. Trade-Tech served as our example of a college emphasizing occupational skills training.

Large maximum values also appear in Table 7.3 for individual fields of study. For colleges in single-campus districts, 31.2 percent of credits completed at Feather River College are in agriculture technology, and fully 63.7 percent of credits completed at Imperial Valley College are in other services. Feather River College is one of three community colleges serving the NorTEC Consortium in the Sierra Nevada mountains of northern California, and Imperial Valley College is near the Mexican border in southern California. Among colleges in multicampus districts, large maximum values include 48.5 percent of credits completed in business at Irvine Valley College, 43.7 percent of credits completed in information technology at Coastline Community College, 40 percent of credits completed in engineering technology at Alameda College, 33.2 percent of credits completed in fashion and child development at Los Angeles Mission College, and 59.0 percent of credits completed in other services at East Los Angeles College. Coastline Community College and Alameda College are located in Orange County and the city of Oakland, respectively.[4]

Inter-quartile ranges shown in Table 7.3 tend to be much smaller than ranges between maximums and minimums. For the voc-ed credits ratio, IQ ranges are 5.7 percentage points for colleges in single-campus districts and 7.8 percentage points for colleges in multicampus districts. Among colleges in single-campus districts, that is, 50 percent of colleges (those in the second and third quartiles) differ from one another by at most 5.7 percentage points in their voc-ed credits ratio. Turning to major fields of study, the table indicates generally modest differences of roughly 2–8 percentage points between colleges in the first and fourth quartiles. Nevertheless, more substantial variation appears for particular fields of study. For other services, the IQ range is 14.0 percentage points and 16.7 percentage points, respectively, for colleges in single-campus and multicampus districts. Large IQ ranges are also found for information technology for colleges in single-campus districts (9.7 percentage points) and engineering technology for colleges in multicampus districts (11.4 percentage points). Inter-quartile ranges for major fields of study tend to be larger for colleges in multicampus districts than colleges in single-campus districts, except for agriculture technology, information technology, and construction crafts, where the opposite is true. Similarly, the IQ range for the proportion of voc-ed credits to all credits is larger for colleges in multicampus districts.

Table 7.3 measures variation in credits supplied by colleges in multicampus districts across districts. To get a feel for variation *within* districts, Table 7.4 shows maximum and minimum values for California's largest district—the Los Angeles CC District. For purposes of comparison, we also show maximum and minimum values for California's two largest counties—Los Angeles County and Orange County. The table shows that variation for the nine colleges in the Los Angeles CC district essentially captures the variation observed for all 21 colleges in L.A. County. For example, the range between maximum and minimum values for the ratio of voc-ed credits to all credits is 33.4 percentage points at the district level as opposed to an only slightly larger 35.2 percentage points for the county. Indeed, a comparison of Table 7.4 with Table 7.3 indicates that much of the variation shown for all 55 colleges in multicampus districts across all of California is accounted for by the nine colleges in the Los Angeles CC district. For example, the range calculated for other services for the Los Angeles CC district of 58.3 percentage points is virtually identical to the 59.0-percentage point range shown in Table 7.3 for all multicampus district colleges. Sizable range values are also calculated for the eight colleges serving Orange County,

Table 7.4 Variation in the Supply of Occupational Training Provided by Community Colleges in the Los Angeles CC District, Los Angeles County, and Orange County (%)

Supply-side variable	Los Angeles CC district (N = 9)		Los Angeles County (N = 21)		Orange County (N = 8)	
	Minimum	Maximum	Minimum	Maximum	Minimum	Maximum
Voc-ed credits/all credits	21.3	54.7	19.5	54.7	18.0	34.5
Occupational distribution of credits						
Agriculture technology	0.0	8.3	0.0	8.3	0.0	4.1
Business	10.9	30.1	9.2	34.3	19.1	48.5
Communications	0.3	9.3	0.3	11.5	0.0	12.0
Information technology	5.9	19.9	3.5	20.5	4.1	43.7
Engineering technology	1.4	23.8	1.4	24.2	3.4	23.5
Construction crafts	0.0	16.1	0.0	16.1	0.0	2.5
Commercial arts	0.1	7.3	0.0	11.0	0.1	7.8
Health care	0.0	12.6	0.0	12.6	0.1	24.3
Fashion and child development	6.1	33.2	1.2	33.2	0.0	10.4
Food and hospitality	0.0	7.5	0.0	7.5	0.0	5.9
Commercial services	0.0	10.5	0.0	17.3	0.0	12.1
Other services	0.7	59.0	0.7	59.0	0.0	30.5

particularly in information technology but also in business, engineering technology, health care, and other services.

VARIATION IN THE DEMAND FOR SKILLS

As noted earlier in this chapter, labor demand data are provided online by the Labor Market Information Division of California's Employment Development Department. Working in cooperation with the CCCS Chancellor's Office, LMID developed this data set to provide community colleges with information to more accurately forecast local demand for occupational skills. We begin this section by describing LMID measures of estimated employment in 1999 and projected new jobs over the interval 1999–2006, where new jobs are defined as the sum of job growth plus labor force separations. Projected new jobs data are used to construct our measure of local labor demand. Note the overlap between the six-year interval over which the supply of new skills is measured (1996–2002) and the eight-year interval over which labor demand is projected (1999–2006).

Both estimated employment and projected new jobs are classified by four-digit TOP codes and are available by county. As described in the first section of this chapter, there are 35 observations (31 counties plus four consortia) for which we can calculate the occupational distributions of employment and projected job opportunities. For the three representative colleges discussed in the second section, we already noted that Santa Monica City College and Los Angeles Trade-Tech College are located in the same county, Los Angeles County, while Santa Barbara City College is located in Santa Barbara County. Table 7.5 describes for these two counties the occupational distributions of estimated 1999 employment and projected new jobs over the 1999–2006 period using the same TOP code classification scheme employed in the second section. Columns (1) and (3) express 1999 employment in each occupational category as a percentage of estimated total employment measured over all TOP codes for which we have estimated employment. For both counties, 1999 employment is seen to be proportionately largest in business, followed at some distance by engineering technology, health care, and food and hospitality.

Table 7.5 Estimated 1999 Employment and Projected New Jobs for 1999–2006, by Occupation, LMID Estimates and Projections, Los Angeles and Santa Barbara Counties (%)

	Los Angeles County		Santa Barbara County	
Occupation	Employment (1)	Share of new jobs (2)	Employment (3)	Share of new jobs (4)
Agriculture technology	1.3	1.5	2.3	2.8
Business	39.2	35.5	35.2	32.4
Communications	0.5	0.7	0.4	0.4
Information technology	1.6	2.4	1.5	2.2
Engineering technology	18.0	15.9	20.1	20.0
Construction crafts	2.4	3.1	2.7	2.9
Commercial arts	1.2	1.2	1.0	0.9
Health care	12.6	12.7	11.6	11.8
Fashion and child development	3.1	1.2	1.6	1.1
Food and hospitality	8.8	12.2	11.5	13.8
Commercial services	4.8	4.7	4.3	3.4
Other services	6.5	8.8	7.6	8.3

We use LMID labor demand projections over the 1999–2006 period to calculate a measure of occupational labor demand that we refer to as *share of new jobs*. Again focusing on L.A. and Santa Barbara Counties, this measure, shown in columns (2) and (4) of Table 7.5, is the number of new job opportunities in each occupational category expressed as a proportion of total projected new jobs. For example, 35.5 percent of new jobs in Los Angeles County are projected to require training in business. The table shows, in both Los Angeles and Santa Barbara Counties, that new jobs are expected to be the most plentiful in business, followed by engineering technology, health care, and food and hospitality. Comparing columns (1) and (2) and columns (3) and (4), shares of expected new jobs in L.A. County and Santa Barbara County are quite similar to shares of existing 1999 jobs. The occupations that are projected to exhibit the fastest growth in both counties are information technology (albeit from a small base) and food and hospitality

Measured across the 31 counties and four labor market consortia, Table 7.6 describes new job projections over the 1999–2006 period classified by major occupational TOP codes. Average share of projected new jobs is largest in business followed at a distance by engineering technology, food and hospitality, health care, and other services. Notice that employment projections are not available for all 35 counties and consortia for communications and commercial arts. Even for those counties and consortia for which data are available, average shares of projected new jobs are very small for these occupational fields at 0.4 percent for communications and 0.6 percent for commercial arts.

Table 7.6 shows that variation in projected shares, as measured by maximum/minimum range, is largest for jobs in engineering technology, other services, food and hospitality, and information technology. For engineering technology, for example, the range is 12.8 percentage points calculated as the difference between a 24.5 percent share of projected new jobs for Tulare County and a share of projected new jobs of just 11.7 percent for Monterey County. Comparing maximum/minimum ranges and IQ ranges across occupational categories, the much smaller IQ ranges indicate that most of the variation in the distributions is at the extremes. Continuing to focus on engineering technology, for example, the IQ range is just 4.2 percentage points. One further point of interest concerns information technology. Note that while for most counties the share of projected new jobs in this occupation is small, there are a few counties for which this is not the case. In particular, a sizeable 9.4 percent of new jobs in information technology is projected for Santa Clara County. Recall from Chapter 6 that Santa Clara County (along with Orange County) was identified as having a heavy concentration of Asian immigrant residents.

Before we bring together our supply-side and demand-side measures, it is perhaps unnecessary to mention that critical to the successful application of our matching approach is an accurate measure of new jobs at the local level. On its Web site, California's Employment Development Department (2005) provides documentation that increases our confidence that using local area occupational demand projections makes sense. Three points are relevant. First, EDD notes that the demand projections are developed in cooperation with the CCCS Chancellor's Office and are explicitly intended to provide information on the job outlook for students in occupational education programs. Second, the methodology used appears quite reasonable. The LMID conducts annual surveys of employers and derives industry occupation-

Table 7.6 Descriptive Statistics for Projected New Jobs by Occupation, Calculated over Counties and Labor Market Consortia (%)

Share of projected growth by occupation	Mean	Minimum	Maximum	Inter-quartile range
Agriculture technology	2.3	1.0	3.8	0.9
Business	33.0	29.3	37.9	2.6
Communications[a]	0.4	0.1	1.3	0.1
Information technology	2.2	0.3	9.4	2.4
Engineering technology	18.4	11.7	24.5	4.2
Construction crafts	3.6	1.9	7.0	2.0
Commercial arts[b]	0.6	0.0	1.3	0.3
Health care	12.2	9.1	18.1	2.3
Fashion and child development	0.8	−0.4	1.4	0.1
Food and hospitality	13.4	9.4	19.1	3.8
Commercial services	3.6	2.2	4.9	1.1
Other services	9.6	5.6	16.0	3.4

NOTE: $N = 35$.

[a] Data are available for 31 counties.

[b] Data are available for 30 counties.

al staffing patterns from the survey results. Labor Market Information Division personnel then apply the staffing patterns to their estimates of current and projected industry employment. Estimation procedures take into account technology and demographic factors that are likely to affect occupation employment during the time frame examined. Third, EDD suggests that LMID demand projections are suitable for carrying out interarea comparisons of county and regional occupational labor demand.

It should also be mentioned, however, that EDD indicates three reasons for caution in using the employment demand projections. While we believe that these reasons do not rule out our use of the projections, they should at least be noted. First, employment projections should most appropriately be used as approximations of actual employment counts. Second, projections cannot reflect labor market events such as firms going out of business, entry of new employers, and military base closures that have occurred since projections were made. Finally, occupational totals are annual averages and, as such, may understate the actual number of workers employed in seasonal activities such as food processing, construction, and tourism.

For further evidence on the accuracy of LMID local area labor demand projections, we were able to contact Carl Hedlind, manager of the LMID Projections Unit. In an extended e-mail exchange, Mr. Hedlind supplied us additional information supporting the accuracy and usefulness of LMID projections. Some of the highlights of this discussion include the following:

- Preliminary local area projections are assessed by LMID local labor market consultants who are familiar with changes in the local economy that analysts in Sacramento may not be aware of.

- LMID staff recently put together a handbook to assist community college officials in using the labor market projections to evaluate the need for new training programs.

- National projections furnished by the Bureau of Labor Statistics (BLS) are a major factor in the development of California projections, and the state follows the BLS cycle for developing new projections. Furthermore, state projections are reviewed by BLS staff members to look for outliers. Mr. Hedlind notes that in most cases, deviations of California projections from national projections are due to some of the unique industries in the state (e.g., viticulture or motion pictures), and revisions of California data have not been required.

ASSESSING THE QUALITY OF SKILL MATCHES

Measuring Labor Market Responsiveness

Based on the familiar Duncan Index widely used in studies of discrimination, our primary tool for measuring a college's labor market responsiveness is a measure we term responsiveness (R). For a particular community college, R is written as

$$(7.1) \quad R = 100 - (\tfrac{1}{2} \Sigma \, | \, S_i - D_i \, |).$$

Expressed in terms of variables included in our data set, S_i is the percentage of credits completed in occupational field of study i by the members of the 1996 FTF cohort over the 1996–2002 time period, and D_i is the percentage of projected new jobs in occupation i in the local labor market over the 1999–2006 time period. The absolute value of the differences in proportions is summed over occupational fields of study and divided by 2. The quantity in parentheses potentially ranges from 0 to 100 percent, with 0 indicating a perfect match between labor demand and supply across all fields of study, and 100 percent indicating the unlikely scenario of all students receiving training in fields of study for which there is zero projected labor demand. As a final step, we subtract the quantity in parentheses from 100 so that higher values of R indicate greater similarity between student training and projected new jobs, and hence a higher level of community college responsiveness.

It is useful to develop the underlying intuition of the $S - D$ differences appearing in Equation (7.1). Our aim is to compare the addition to the stock of occupational skills supplied by a community college to its labor market with local employers' need for additional skilled workers. We view both S and D as representing flows of human capital to the community. On the supply side, we follow a cohort of FTF students over a six-year period. The skills they acquire represent an addition to the total stock of skills available to the community. On the demand side, projected new jobs represent an addition to the stock of existing jobs in the local labor market.

If we had data on newly trained workers, we could match in Equation (7.1) the number of trained workers with the number of newly created jobs. This comparison would provide a measure that might be termed a college's *absolute* labor market responsiveness. One way to visualize the concept of absolute responsiveness is a scenario in which a local reporter asks a community college president what the college is doing to respond to reports of a large number of new jobs in an occupation. If the college is absolute labor market responsive, the president's response would be that the college is committed to providing trained workers to fill some fraction of these new jobs, where the specified fraction hinges on the size of the college in relation to the labor market.

In contrast, our data allow us to take a less exacting *relative* responsiveness approach, by which we mean that a labor market–responsive community college will respond to a perceived shift in labor demand by allocating new resources and reallocating existing resources so that student credits completed increase in high-demand fields of study at the expense of credits completed in low-demand fields. Consequently, a market-responsive college's occupational distribution of credits completed will be observed to move towards the occupational distribution of new jobs in the local labor market. In response to the reporter's question posed above, that is, the president of a relative-labor-market-responsive college would be expected to answer that the college is shifting resources toward high-demand fields of study and away from training in other fields.

To illustrate how our responsiveness measure works (Table 7.7), consider the College A and College B example back in the first section making two modifications. First, assume that there are three, rather than two, major fields of study. Second, rather than Colleges A and B being in the same labor market, assume that they are in two different labor markets.

As seen in Table 7.7, there is a fairly close match for College A between percentages of additional credits earned in the three fields of study and the percentages of new jobs in corresponding occupations. Applying the responsiveness formula yields R = 90 percent. Since R = 100 percent captures a perfect match between labor demand and supply, an R value of 90 percent indicates that College A should be viewed as highly responsive to local labor market conditions. The scenario changes for College B. As is true for College A, half of the second college's students prepare for a career in food and hospitality. However, projected labor demand indicates that only 5 percent of new jobs will require training in this occupation. Instead, the major category of new jobs in this labor market is engineering technology. We calculate that R = 40

Table 7.7 Illustration Contrasting Two Hypothetical Colleges that Differ in their Labor Market Responsiveness (%)

Occupation	College A		College B	
	Supply	Demand	Supply	Demand
Engineering technology	25	33	25	85
Health care	25	27	25	10
Food and hospitality	50	40	50	5
Responsiveness	90		40	

Table 7.8 Estimates of Responsiveness for Community Colleges at the Levels of the Individual College and CC District (%)

Level of aggregation	Mean	Minimum	Maximum	Inter-quartile range
All 106 colleges	60.1	32.4	81.7	12.6
All 71 districts	62.3	42.5	82.1	12.4

percent, indicating that College B is much less labor market responsive than College A.

Matching by College

Table 7.8 presents calculated R values using, for each occupation, shares of additional credits completed to represent the supply side and shares of projected new jobs to represent the demand side. Since projected new jobs are not available for the fields of communications and commercial arts for all 35 counties and consortia, we calculate R over the 10 occupations for which we have data for all 35 counties and consortia. The first section in this chapter described two approaches to matching supply of trained workers with local employers' demand for skills. The first of these involves matching supply at the college level with county/consortia demand, and the first row of Table 7.8 shows the results of implementing this approach. The (unweighted) average value of R over all 106 colleges in our data set is 60.1 percent, with a substantial range between maximum and minimum estimates of 49.3 percentage points and a large IQ range of 12.6 percentage points. The maximum R value of 81.7 percent is obtained for Mission College and the minimum of 32.4 percent for East Los Angeles College. Recall from Table 7.1 that Mission College is located in Santa Clara County on the San Francisco Bay Peninsula, and East Los Angeles College is part of the nine-campus Los Angeles CC District. We noted in the previous section that Santa Clara County has a heavy concentration of Asian immigrants, and Chapter 6 pointed out that Mission College is one of only a handful of California community colleges with a high proportion of Vietnamese students.

Table 7.9 goes into detail on the quality of the matches calculated for Mission College and East Los Angeles College. The table shows that Mission College comes very close to matching the shares of pro-

Table 7.9 Detailed Comparison by Occupation of Labor Demand and
Supply for Mission College and East Los Angeles College (%)

	Mission College		East L.A. College	
Occupation	Supply	Demand	Supply	Demand
Agriculture technology	0.3	1.5	0.0	1.6
Business	27.6	32.4	11.2	36.2
Information technology	11.8	9.5	6.3	2.5
Engineering technology	26.3	21.7	3.4	16.2
Construction crafts	0.0	3.8	0.0	3.2
Health care	12.5	10.5	4.5	13.0
Fashion and child development	1.7	0.5	13.5	1.3
Food and hospitality	5.3	9.5	0.5	12.4
Commercial services	0.0	4.2	0.0	4.7
Other services	14.4	6.3	60.5	9.0

jected new jobs in Santa Clara County in business and engineering technology, the two fields of study with the largest shares of projected new jobs (32.4 percent and 21.7 percent, respectively). Notice also that Mission College's supply of credits completed in information technology closely matches the Santa Clara County demand in this field (9.5 percent). What makes these findings for engineering technology and information technology especially noteworthy is that projected levels of new jobs in these two fields are considerably above statewide levels of slightly over 2 percent for information technology and 18.4 percent for engineering technology (see Table 7.6). The only field of study for which Mission College fails to match demand closely is other services. Mission College supplies 14.4 percent of credits completed in other services, whereas the share of new jobs in this field in Santa Clara County is projected to be only 6.3 percent.

Measured across occupations, new credits completed at East Los Angeles College, on the other hand, consistently fall short of projected demand for Los Angeles County. The one exception to this statement is the field of other services, where added supply greatly exceeds projected demand. As noted earlier in connection with Table 7.3, East Los Angeles College supplies the largest share of total credits completed in other services of any college in a multicollege CC district.[5]

We introduced in Chapter 4 a study by Jacobson et al. (2005, Appendix C) that is part of the U.S. Department of Education's Community College Labor Market Responsiveness Initiative. This study furnishes some useful background for interpreting Tables 7.8 and 7.9. The authors link college-specific data drawn from the Integrated Postsecondary Education Data System (IPEDS) to Census Bureau and Bureau of Labor Statistics information on community demographics and local labor market characteristics. Using this matched data set, community colleges found to be labor market responsive can be characterized in terms of the following factors.

1. Large enrollments. Jacobson et al. (2005) explain that large enrollments are indicators of 1) the administrative resources to design, fund, and implement career-oriented programs; and 2) programs likely to form the basis of partnerships with local businesses and economic development agencies.

2. Large budgets with a substantial local government contribution. The authors suggest that local government funding presents a "buy-in" from local civic and business leaders that help colleges focus on meeting local education and training needs.

3. Suburban location. Finally, they argue that a location in the suburbs of a major metropolitan area is important because of the likely proximity of the college to large high-tech employers and associated partnership opportunities.

Jacobson et al. suggest that these factors should be viewed as external constraints on how easy or difficult it is for a college to develop market-responsive programs. They caution, however, that it is quite common for colleges with substantial external capacity to fail to reach their potential. Conversely, it is common for colleges that appear to have a modest capacity to overachieve in their market responsiveness.

With this background, we list in Table 7.10 the top-five colleges, led by Mission College, and the bottom-five colleges, led by East Los Angeles College, measured in terms of responsiveness. In addition to R scores, we compare these two categories of colleges with respect to their district affiliation and key labor market responsiveness characteristics. There does not appear to be an important distinction between single-campus and multicampus district colleges. All 10 colleges shown are members of multicampus districts, with the exception of Santa

Table 7.10 Characteristics of Colleges with High R Scores and Colleges with Low R Scores

College	R score	Location	District affiliation and county	Fall 2001 student headcount (in 000's)	Voc-ed credits ratio	District total revenue per student (in $)	District local share of total revenue, 2001–02 (%)
Top five							
Mission	81.7	Santa Clara on the S.F. Bay Peninsula just west of San Jose	One of 2 colleges in the West Valley–Mission district. Seven colleges serve Santa Clara County.	11.8	0.333	3,321	65.5
Santa Barbara City	79.2	Santa Barbara	Only college in Santa Barbara district. Two colleges serve Santa Barbara County.	14.9	0.204	4,431	35.5
San Mateo	76.9	San Mateo on the S.F. Bay Peninsula just south of S.F.	One of 3 colleges in the San Mateo County district serving San Mateo County	11.9	0.265	3,952	79.2
Saddleback	76.2	Mission Viejo in Orange County	One of 2 colleges in South Orange County district. Eight colleges serve Orange County.	23.4	0.216	3,366	82.5
Skyline	75.0	San Bruno on the S.F. Bay Peninsula just south of S.F.	One of 3 colleges in the San Mateo County district serving San Mateo County	9.0	0.242	3,952	79.2
Bottom five							
East Los Angeles	32.4	Monterey Park in East Los Angeles section of L.A.	One of 9 colleges in the L.A. district	29.2	0.365	3,135	32.7

Merritt	38.3	Oakland	One of 4 colleges in the Peralta district. Seven colleges serve Alameda County.	7.1	0.381	3,425	39.8
Vista	38.6	Berkeley	One of 4 colleges in the Peralta district. Seven colleges serve Alameda County.	4.3	0.195	3,425	39.8
Los Angeles Mission	40.6	Sylmar in the San Fernando Valley	One of 9 colleges in the L.A. district	8.3	0.265	3,135	32.7
Porterville	41.2	Porterville in central California, south of Fresno and north of Bakersfield	One of 3 colleges in the Kern district. It is located in Tulare County.	4.8	0.294	3,702	45.5
Statewide				14.5	0.279	3,772	42.0

SOURCE: Student headcount reported by the California Postsecondary Education Commission and collected in Gill and Leigh (2004). District total revenue and local share Chancellor's Office (n.d., Table IV.1).

Barbara City College.[6] Santa Barbara City College comprises its own district. Two of the other top-five colleges are members of the same district. San Mateo College and Skyline College belong to the San Mateo County CC district. Among the bottom-five colleges, all are part of multicampus districts and four are members of the same two districts. Merritt College and Vista College belong to the Peralta CC district serving Alameda County, and East Los Angeles College and Los Angeles Mission College are part of the Los Angeles CC district.

Colleges that are heavily oriented toward vocational training as measured by the voc-ed credits ratio might reasonably be expected to be more labor market responsive than other colleges. Nevertheless, Table 7.10 fails to indicate a clear-cut difference between top-five and bottom-five colleges. Mission College in the top-five category reports a voc-ed credits ratio of 33.3 percent, but ratios calculated for East Los Angeles College and Merritt College in the bottom five are even higher at 36.5 percent and 38.1 percent, respectively.

More important distinctions between top-five and bottom-five colleges appear with respect to the external constraint factors discussed by Jacobson et al. (2005). Beginning with enrollment, top-five colleges tend to be midsize or large, topping out with Saddleback College's enrollment of over 23,000 students. In contrast, bottom-five colleges are well below statewide average enrollment of about 14,500 students, with the exception of the very large East Los Angeles College.

The second factor listed by Jacobson et al. (2005) is large budgets with a substantial local government buy-in. Table 7.10 displays measures of total revenue per student and share of local to total revenue, each measured at the district level. With the exception of Santa Barbara City College, there is a clear distinction between top-five and bottom-five colleges with respect to the local revenue ratio. Saddleback College in the South Orange CC district and San Mateo College and Skyline College in the San Mateo CC district, in particular, enjoy a very high ratio of local to total revenue. On the other hand, SBCC reports a local revenue ratio that is below the statewide average of 42.0 percent. Among bottom-five colleges, only Porterville College ranks above the statewide average.

Top-five colleges also tend to enjoy a higher level of total revenue per student, although the difference between top-five and bottom-five colleges is not as striking as it is in the case of local revenue share.

Especially noteworthy among top-five colleges is the relatively high per student revenue estimate shown for Santa Barbara City College ($4,431). Among bottom-five colleges, Porterville College reports the highest total revenue per student of $3,702.

Consistent with the third factor mentioned by Jacobson et al. (2005), a suburban location appears to be an important consideration in distinguishing top-five from bottom-five colleges. Among the top five, Mission, San Mateo, and Skyline Colleges are located in prosperous suburban areas on the San Francisco Bay Peninsula, and Saddleback College is likewise located in a prosperous suburban area of Orange County. To get a better idea of how the communities in which these top-five colleges are located compare in terms of average income, we checked median household income estimates for 1999 taken from the 2000 census and reported in Gill and Leigh (2004). Median household income estimates range from about $62,000 for the city of San Bruno (Skyline College) to over $78,000 for the city of Mission Viejo (Saddleback College). These estimates are well above the California statewide average of $49,000. Mission, San Mateo, and Skyline Colleges are also located in close geographic proximity to the high-tech Silicon Valley area centered near Stanford University in Palo Alto. At slightly over $47,000, median household income for the city of Santa Barbara is essentially at the statewide average.

In contrast to the largely suburban character of the top-five schools, bottom-five colleges tend to be located in either urban or rural areas. East Los Angeles College and Los Angeles Mission College are located in the city of Los Angeles, while Merritt College and Vista College service the cities of Oakland and Berkeley, respectively. The fifth of the bottom-five colleges, Porterville College, is located in a rural area in California's Central Valley. Median household income estimates for bottom-five colleges range between $32,000 for Porterville College in the city of Porterville and $44,000 for Vista College in Berkeley.

Matching by District

How do our results change when we perform the same analysis at the district rather than the individual college level? We noted in the first section that California community colleges are organized administratively into districts. This raises the possibility that multicollege districts coordinate their vocational curriculums in order to increase district-wide labor market responsiveness. If this is the case, the proper level for evaluating responsiveness is the district rather than the individual college.

To gain a better understanding of the level at which important resource allocation decisions are made, we contacted Willard Hom, director of the Research and Planning Unit in the CCCS Chancellor's Office. Mr. Hom in turn contacted Charles Klein, a curriculum staff specialist in the Research and Planning Unit, on our behalf. In the key area of curriculum decisions, Messrs. Hom and Klein indicate that districts display considerable heterogeneity. Many districts maintain a districtwide curriculum committee, but the authority of this committee over individual colleges in the district varies. At one extreme, Hom and Klein explain that the committee operating in the Los Angeles CC District exercises considerable direct control and often second-guesses the curriculum committees of individual member campuses. In other districts, the district committee serves a coordinating and information-sharing function rather than an approval function. Still other districts have no district-wide curriculum committee at all.

To examine the possibility that the efforts of individual colleges are coordinated at the district level, we calculate our responsiveness measure for the 71 districts included in our data set. Our approach is as follows. Recall from Equation (7.1) that for a particular college we sum over occupational fields of study the absolute value of the difference between that college's share of new credits completed in field i (S_i) and the share of new jobs in field i in the county in which the college is located (D_i). To move to the district level, S_i becomes, for multicollege districts, a weighted average of the shares of member colleges of credits completed in field i. Weights applied are the proportion of each college's enrollment to total district enrollment. In principle, the R score calculated for a particular district might either exceed or fall short of R calculated for a member community college.

To clarify this point, consider the example in the first section of two colleges comprising a community college district and two fields of study—engineering technology and health care. Suppose that both colleges have low R values because they choose to specialize—College A specializes in engineering technology by supplying a larger share of engineering technology credits than the share of new jobs at the market level. At the same time, it undershoots market demand in health care. College B chooses to specialize in health care and does just the opposite—that is, it overshoots market demand in health care and undershoots demand in engineering technology. Because the two colleges' specializations are complementary, the district-level R value exceeds R calculated for either college individually.

On the other hand, the district-level R value might fall below that of one or more member colleges. Consider two cases. Case 1 focuses on the situation in which the two colleges compete with, rather than complement, each other by offering the same curriculum specialization. If both colleges specialize in engineering technology, for example, R calculated for one college will be dragged down at the district level by a lower R value for the other, which is even more specialized than the first college. In Case 2, suppose that College A has a high R score because it successfully mimics demand across most fields of study. If the second college in the district is less successful at mimicking demand, its lower level of market responsiveness will dilute that of the first causing R calculated at the district level to fall below that of College A.

Table 7.8 indicates that the mean R score calculated across districts is 2.2 percentage points higher than the mean R score for colleges. This result is almost entirely due to a minimum R score at the district level that is higher by 10.1 percentage points than the minimum R score calculated for colleges. Recall that the bottom-five colleges in Table 7.10 are all members of multicampus districts. The observations that the bottom-five colleges are all in multicollege districts and that, as seen in Table 7.11, none of the bottom-five districts are multicollege districts suggests that colleges that appear to score poorly in terms of labor market responsiveness are often matched in multicampus districts with other colleges in such a way that overall district performance increases. This might occur for either of two reasons. First, the first college's low R score is due to specialization, and other colleges in the district offer complementary specializations. Second, the first college is matched in its district with one or more colleges that do a better job of mimicking local labor market demand.

Evidence on districts at both ends of the R-score distribution is presented in Table 7.11. Top-five districts in this table come close to mirroring the top-five colleges described earlier. The San Mateo County CC district is the most labor market responsive of all 71 districts, a

Table 7.11 Characteristics of Districts with High R Scores and Districts with Low R Scores

District	R score	Location	District affiliation and county	District fall 2001 student headcount (000)	District total revenue per student ($)	District local share of total revenue, 2001–02 (%)
Top five						
San Mateo County	82.1	S.F. Bay Peninsula just west of San Jose	Three colleges in district (Canada, San Mateo, and Skyline) serve San Mateo County	27.0	3,952	79.2
Santa Barbara	79.2	Pacific coast north of Los Angeles	Single-college district. Two single-college districts serve Santa Barbara County.	14.9	4,431	35.5
South Orange	76.4	Southern part of Orange County	Two colleges (Irvine Valley and Saddleback) in district. Eight colleges in 4 districts serve Orange County.	35.3	3,366	82.5
San Diego	75.7	City of San Diego	Three colleges in district (S.D. City, S.D. Mesa, and S.D. Miramar). Seven colleges in 4 districts serve San Diego County.	46.7	4,807	37.8
Glendale	74.8	Northwest of central Los Angeles	Single-college district. Thirteen districts serve L.A. County.	23.0	3,132	38.1
Bottom five						
Imperial	42.5	Southeast corner of the state just north of the Mexican border	Single-college district serving Imperial County	7.1	4,067	26.4

Feather River	44.0	Lightly populated area north of Sacramento	Single-college district. One of 3 colleges in 3 districts serving the NorTEC Consortium	2.0	5,649	34.0
Compton	46.0	Central Los Angeles	Single-college district. Thirteen districts serve L.A. County.	10.4	3,339	24.7
Rio Hondo	47.1	Just east of central Los Angeles	Single-college district. Thirteen districts serve L.A. County.	18.6	3,535	30.5
Napa Valley	48.0	North and east of San Francisco	Single-college district serving Napa County	9.4	3,332	54.7
Statewide				21.8	3,772	42.0

SOURCE: Student headcount reported by the California Postsecondary Education Commission and collected in Gill and Leigh (2004). District total revenue and local share are from Chancellor's Office (n.d., Table IV.1).

result that is not surprising since member colleges San Mateo College and Skyline College rank third and fifth, respectively, in the top-five labor market-responsive colleges. But it is noteworthy that the R score for this district of 82.1 percent is higher than the R scores for either San Mateo College (76.9 percent) or Skyline College (75.0 percent). That is, the two member colleges appear to complement each other in their curriculum offerings as well as complementing the third college in the district. (The third member college is Canada College with an R score of 56.2 percent.)

The Santa Barbara CC district, a single-college district, is in second place on the district ranking, as is Santa Barbara City College on the college ranking. The South Orange CC district, ranked third in Table 7.11, includes fourth-ranked Saddleback College on the individual college ranking. In fourth place is the San Diego CC district with a R score of 75.7 percent, even though none of the three colleges comprising this district make it into the top-five performing colleges. Member colleges (and their R scores) are San Diego City College (62.5 percent), San Diego Mesa College (71.6 percent), and San Diego Miramar College (53.5 percent).

The Glendale CC district rounds out the top five. As a single-college district, Glendale College's R score of 74.8 percent would rank it just below fifth-place Skyline College among top-five colleges. First ranked Mission College in Table 7.10 is a member of the West Valley–Mission CC district, for which we calculate an R score of 74.7 percent. This R score would place the West Valley–Mission district just below the top-five rated districts. Hence, Mission College appears to be the only case among top-five colleges in which a member college dilutes the responsiveness, measured at the district level, of a highly labor market–responsive college. This result reflects a common-sense property of a mean, that is, a very high R score is likely to be dragged down when the college is combined with other colleges in its district that, by definition, have lower R scores.

Turning to the bottom-five districts in Table 7.11, note that all five districts are single-college districts. This result contrasts strongly with the bottom-five colleges described in Table 7.10, all of which are members of multicampus districts. In other words, all of the low R-score colleges in Table 7.10 are combined with other colleges in their districts in such a way that no multicampus district appears among the bottom-five districts. For this to happen, member colleges must be either colleges that offer complementary specializations or higher-performing colleges. The second of these reasons is the property of an average just noted. Evidence that the first reason is at least a possibility is found for the four-college Peralta CC district. In Table 7.10, member colleges Merritt College and Vista College rank second and third from the bottom, respectively, in terms of their individual R scores (38.3 percent and 38.6 percent, respectively). Within the Peralta CC district, these two colleges are combined with higher-scoring Alameda College (R = 59.9 percent) and Laney College (R = 64.1 percent). But rather than its score lying between the scores for the individual member colleges, the Peralta CC district score is 70.5 percent, considerably above the highest score of member colleges and close to the score that would put it among the top-five districts.

In addition to location and type of district, Table 7.11 compares top-five and bottom-five districts with respect to district enrollment, revenue per student, and share of local revenue to total revenues. Top-five districts appear to be larger in terms of enrollment and to have a larger share of local revenues. On the other hand, there does not seem to be much difference between the two categories of districts with respect to total revenue per student.

Regression Results

To generalize on the comparisons illustrated in Tables 7.10 and 7.11, we estimate a simple regression model to use as a tool for predicting the capacity of a community college to provide a labor market-responsive range of programs. Drawing on evidence supplied by Jacobson et al. (2005, Appendix C), the model takes the following form:

$$\text{R-SCORE} = b_0 + b_1\text{MULTICAMPUS} + b_2\text{ENROLL} + b_3\text{REV/CAPITA}$$
$$+ b_4\text{LOCAL-REV} + b_5\text{VOC-ED} + u,$$

where explanatory variables are defined as follows:

MULTICAMPUS = 1 if college is part of a multicollege district, 0 otherwise;

ENROLL = college's fall 2001 student headcount (in thousands);

REV/CAPITA = district total revenue per student measured in 2001–02 (in thousands of dollars);

LOCAL-REV = district ratio of local to total revenue, 2001–02;

VOC-ED = college's ratio of voc-ed credits to all credits; and

u = an error term.

Regression estimates obtained for this model at the individual college level appear in column (1) of Table 7.12.[7]

Based on impressions formed earlier from Table 7.10, the absence of statistically significant effects in column (1) of the multicampus dummy variable and the voc-ed credits ratio are not unexpected. On the other hand, the three measures of fiscal capacity all have the anticipated sign and are statistically significant. The magnitudes of these effects, however, are not terribly large. A 10-percentage-point increase in the local revenue share increases a college's R score by about 1.3 percentage points. Similarly, moving from a small to a large college by increasing enrollment by 10,000 students increases a college's predicted R score by 3.2 percentage points. Finally, increasing total revenue per student by $1,000, a very large increase, raises the predicted R score by just 3.13 percentage points. In terms of predicting a particular college's R score, the modest R^2 statistic of 0.16 indicates that our predictions are unlikely to be very accurate. We view this evidence as consistent with the conjecture of Jacobson et al. (2005) that while external constraints are important, they are not sufficient to provide an accurate prediction of a particular college's labor market responsiveness.

Column (2) of Table 7.12 supplies estimates of the effects of these variables in a regression determining district-level R scores. As in column (1), local revenue share is estimated to have a positive and statistically significant effect on labor market responsiveness. Estimated effects of enrollment and revenue per student are no longer statistically significant, however.

The most striking result in column (2) is that, controlling for the effects of external constraint variables, multicampus districts report R scores 5.73 percentage points higher than those for single-campus districts. This contrasts strongly with our column (1) finding that membership in a multicampus district has no significant effect on individual colleges' R scores. We emphasize this result because it is counter to what would be expected from the common-sense property of a mean noted above, that is, a coefficient estimate in column (2) of about zero.

Table 7.12 Regression Estimates of Relationships Determining R Scores for Colleges and Districts

Explanatory variable	Colleges (1)	Districts (2)
Intercept	41.75**	47.22**
	(8.38)	(6.81)
Multicampus district	−0.41	5.73**
	(1.85)	(2.80)
Enrollment (000)[a]	0.32**	0.05
	(0.12)	(0.06)
District revenue per student ($,000)	3.13**	1.74
	(1.44)	(1.48)
District local revenue share	12.77**	13.92*
	(6.64)	(7.16)
College voc-ed credits ratio	−11.63	—
	(14.12)	
R^2	0.16	0.17
N	106	71

NOTE: *Significantly different from zero at the 0.10 level; **significantly different from zero at the 0.05 level. A dash (—) indicates that the variable is omitted from the regression. Standard errors are in parentheses.
[a] Measured for colleges in column (1) and districts in column (2).

It makes sense that the R scores of low-scoring colleges in a multicampus district will be pulled up by the other colleges in their district, which by definition have higher R scores. As a consequence, the multicampus district will have a higher R score than those of its low-scoring member colleges. This upward pressure tends to raise the scores of multicampus districts in comparison to those of single-campus districts.

Just the opposite reasoning holds for districts that include high-scoring colleges. In this case, we would expect that the R scores of these multicampus districts will be drawn down in comparison to high-scoring colleges that comprise their own districts. An example of such a high-scoring college in a multicampus district is Mission College in the West Valley-Mission District. As noted earlier in this section, Mission College's R score is 81.7 percent as compared to a West Valley–Mission district score of 74.7 percent.

Since, as seen in Table 7.10, colleges in multicampus districts appear in both tails of the college R-score distribution, this property of a mean suggests that the coefficient on the multicampus variable in the district regression in column (2) of Table 7.12 should be approximately zero. The reason is that downward pressure on the R scores of multicampus districts including high-scoring colleges would be just offset by upward pressure on the R scores of multicampus districts including low-scoring colleges. On the other hand, the examples of the San Mateo County, San Diego, and Peralta CC districts pointed to in the context of Tables 7.10 and 7.11 raise the possibility of a positive multicampus district effect because coordination of member college curriculum specializations leads to district scores that exceed those of the individual colleges. Rather than being zero, our regression result is that the estimated effect of the multicollege dummy variable approaches 6 percentage points and is statistically significant. This suggests that complementary specialization within multicampus districts is a very real phenomenon among California community colleges.

SUMMARY

This chapter examined the second of two research questions raised in Chapter 1. The question is whether community colleges supply occupational skills training programs that satisfy the changing skill requirements of local employers. We address this question using a new approach to evaluating empirically the concept of labor market responsiveness. The intuition of our approach is simple: labor market–responsive colleges provide training in occupations that matches changes in the demand for skilled workers in the local labor market. Based on this intuition, we evaluate a college's labor market responsiveness by examining how closely its occupational distribution of vocational credits completed by students over the 1996–2002 period, which represent an addition to the stock of skills available to the community, matches the occupational distribution of projected new jobs. Both new vocational credits completed and projected new jobs are classified by the same TOP occupational codes.

On the supply side, we reported substantial variation across 106 community colleges in terms of both emphasis on vocational education curriculums and the occupational distributions of credits completed. On the demand side, data on projected new jobs are available for 31 counties and 4 labor market consortia. Counties also clearly differ in terms of the occupational distributions of projected new jobs.

The quality of the matches between training supplied and local labor demand is assessed using a measure of responsiveness (R). Because California community colleges are organized into districts, we calculate R scores at both the college level and the district level. Across community colleges, R scores vary substantially with the least responsive college receiving a score of 32.4 percent and the most responsive college a score of 81.7 percent. (R scores can range between 1 and 100 percent.) R scores are found to be positively affected by external constraint measures including campus enrollment, revenue per student, share of local revenue in total revenue, and suburban location. Whether a college is a member of a multicampus CC district, however, does not seem to be important. Nor does the emphasis a college places on its voc-ed offerings seem to matter much. We also find that considerable variability in R scores remains even after we control for external constraint measures. Hence, individual colleges appear to differ quite substantially in their responsiveness to local labor demand conditions.

At the district level, we continued to find a positive effect of local revenue share on labor market responsiveness. But otherwise, our district-level results are distinctly different from the college-level findings. For 71 California community college districts, we presented evidence that, holding constant the effects of external constraint variables, multicampus CC districts are more labor market responsive than single-campus districts. Since district R scores combine the scores of individual member colleges, one might expect to find a zero effect for our multicampus dummy variable. Thus, we interpret evidence of a positive effect as supporting the hypothesis, at least within some multicampus districts, that member colleges choose to specialize in their occupational education curriculums, and that these specializations are complementary within districts. In other words, we find that even colleges that, by themselves, would appear to rank low in terms of labor market responsiveness are frequently combined in districts in which member colleges as a group are much more responsive. This result is consistent with the suggestion of staff members in the Chancellor's Office that there is considerable heterogeneity across multicampus districts in the extent of curriculum coordination across individual member colleges.

Notes

1. The FTF data set includes information on 108 community colleges. Of these, we exclude Copper Mountain College and Santiago Canyon College. Copper Mountain College is excluded because it was not founded until 2001. Located in Orange County, Santiago Canyon College in the Rancho Santiago CC district was spun off from Santa Ana College in 1997; it is excluded because complete information is not available. Nevertheless, the Rancho Santiago CC district is a multicampus district, and we treat it as such in the subsequent analysis.

2. The primary deviations from a strict two-digit breakdown of TOP codes are the following: 1) the construction crafts are split off from the other codes included in the two-digit category Engineering Technology (09); 2) we divide the two-digit category Consumer Education and Home Economics (13) into the categories of fashion and child development and food and hospitality; and 3) we lump together in "other services" education, community services, and other miscellaneous services.

3. These statistics are weighted average of means, broken down by gender and race or ethnicity, shown in Table 5.2.

4. Coastline College was singled out in Chapter 6 as one of a handful of community colleges with a heavy enrollment of Vietnamese students.

5. The share of total credits completed in other services by East Los Angeles College appearing in Table 7.3 (59.0 percent) is slightly smaller than that shown in Table 7.9 (60.5) percent because the calculation is performed over 12 occupations in Table 7.3 and just 10 occupations in Table 7.9.

6. As would be expected from its high R score, the data presented earlier in Tables 7.2 and 7.5 indicate a generally close correspondence between the occupational distribution of credits completed at Santa Barbara City College and the occupational distribution of projected new jobs for Santa Barbara County. The only supply-demand differences worth remarking on are that supply exceeds demand for information technology, while supply falls short of projected demand for business and engineering technology.

7. We added median household income to the regression with the result that its parameter estimate was small and statistically insignificant. Coefficient estimates on the other explanatory variables were essentially unchanged.

8
Summary and Policy Implications

This monograph provides an empirical study of the labor market responsiveness of California community colleges. To define what we mean by labor market responsiveness, we borrowed from a definition recently advanced by the U.S. Department of Education's Community College Labor Market Responsiveness Initiative (MacAllum and Yoder 2004). As described in Chapter 1, this definition emphasizes four key aspects of labor market responsiveness. The first is that responsive community colleges react quickly to changing educational and workforce development needs at the local level. Second, these needs span the educational gamut from remedial training to transfer-oriented academic programs. The third aspect is that local labor markets are dynamic because of changes on the supply side as well as on the demand side. Fourth, the dynamic nature of labor markets requires responsive community colleges to look ahead to anticipate future needs of students and employers.

Our study selects for analysis what we believe to be the two major, and policy relevant, sources of change at the local level—one on the supply side and the other on the demand side. On the supply side, we focus on the impact of massive changes in number and national origin of immigrants to the United States over the past 40 years. In contrast to earlier periods in which immigrants were typically European, since the mid-1960s most immigrants have originated from Latin America and Asia. As newcomers to this country, many immigrants need education and training to gain proficiency in English and to acquire the educational background and occupational skills required for higher-level jobs. Community colleges have traditionally served as the point of entry for immigrants into the U.S. system of higher education.

On the demand side, the major source of change is constantly shifting labor demand conditions brought about by ever improving technology and the competitive pressures generated by globalization. Community colleges are the principal institutional provider of training services for youth and adults looking for employment or seeking to upgrade their skills to retain an existing job or qualify for a better job.

Emphasis on these two sources of change leads us to explore the following two questions of contemporary policy concern:

Research Question 1: Are community colleges meeting the education and training needs of current and recent generations of immigrants?

Research Question 2: Do community colleges respond to changing demand conditions by providing occupational training programs that produce skills marketable in the local economy?

In the context of the first question, education and training needs are typically examined in terms of access and outcomes. As described in Chapter 2, California has historically led the nation in access to higher education through the open-admission and low-tuition policies of its community college system and the convenient locations of community college campuses. In our view, the more important question is whether current and recent generations of immigrants benefit from a successful outcome of their community college experiences. Specifically, we compare the educational outcomes of Latino and Asian community college students to those of white students. Chapter 1 emphasized that the Latino-white gap in educational attainment is an important national problem. Latino students are also found to lag behind whites in the community college outcome variables we measure. Our purpose is to identify those barriers at the community college level that appear to underlie the Latino-white gap in educational attainment.

On the other hand, the educational attainment of Asian community college students often exceeds that of white students. For Asians, consequently, we seek to identify those factors that contribute to their superior outcomes. Our goal is to learn from the experience of Asians those lessons that may be useful for helping community colleges better meet the educational needs of other immigrants.

Turning to Research Question 2, we develop a novel methodology to examine the matches, at the local labor market level, between the occupational distribution of skills supplied by community colleges and the occupational distribution of skills demanded by employers. On the supply side, we look at the distribution of vocational credits completed classified by occupational fields of study. Our demand-side measure is based on employment projections classified by the same occupational codes. We define a measure termed *responsiveness* to assess the quality of matches at the local labor market level. Our goal is to better characterize community colleges that are labor market responsive.

We begin by reviewing why we chose data for California community colleges for our empirical analysis. Then in the following two sections, we discuss our results for Research Questions 1 and 2 and point out some policy implications. The last section contains some final thoughts.

CALIFORNIA FIRST-TIME-FRESHMEN DATA

Conceptually, we could explore our two research questions using any one of a number of data sets containing a nationally representative sample of individuals, only a small fraction of which would have enrolled in a community college at some point in their lives. However, our empirical analysis requires us to have information on a large number of community college students—a larger number than is available in any commonly used national data set. In terms of answering Research Question 1, a large number of community college student observations is needed so that we have enough Latino and Asian students for analysis. Research Question 2 also requires data on a large number of community college students because we need a sufficient number of students enrolled in each community college to accurately measure differences across colleges in occupational fields of study.

The alternative to a nationally representative data set is administrative data for the community college system of a particular state. We take this alternative, and the state we selected is California. As outlined in Chapter 1, there are several reasons for this choice. These include California's status as the state that receives more immigrants than any other state, the fact that the California Community College System (CCCS) is by far the largest in the nation, and the massive size of the state's economy. A final, very practical, reason is that we were able to obtain from the Chancellor's Office student records for all first-time freshmen (FTF) attending any CCCS campus in 1996. This cohort of freshmen students is followed over a six-year interval. The large size of the CCCS means that we have over 300,000 observations in our data extract.

From the perspective of answering Research Question 1, FTF data offer a number of advantages. One advantage is that the data provide a rich source of information on individual student characteristics. These include educational background and citizenship status, academic goals upon entering college, academic progress while attending college, and outcomes of students' college experience. In addition, a valuable feature of FTF data is that not only is information available on major categories of race or ethnicity, but detailed categories of national origin are distinguished within the broad Latino and Asian categories. The large number of observations in the FTF data set is crucial for taking full advantage of this level of detail on race or ethnicity. We also know from FTF data the particular CCCS community college attended. This information allows us to do two things. First, we can attach characteristics of the college attended to the record for each student; and, second, we can estimate college-specific fixed effects on educational attainment.

At the same time, there are also some disadvantages of FTF data. One of these, which we have noted at various places in the monograph, is that common measures of family background such as family income, parents' education, and number of siblings are not available in student records. Measures of family background are typically found in national data sets. A second disadvantage, in comparison to the use of national data, is that we are unable to study the decision process that leads some students to attend a community college, while others enroll in four-year institutions and still others opt for immediate employment.

Turning to Research Question 2, FTF data supply information on the credits students complete classified by major field of study along with, as noted, the college attended. This allows us to construct the distribution of new occupational skills supplied over the 1996-2002 period by each community college. As just noted, a large number of observations, such as is available in the FTF data set, is essential to obtain a reasonably accurate representation of the occupational skills supplied by each of the 106 CCCS colleges examined. On the demand side, we match the occupational distribution of skills supplied with employment projections by county using the same breakdown of occupations. These county-level employment projections are provided by the Labor Market Information Division (LMID) of California's Employment Development Department. Our methodology consists of matching a college's distribution of new skills supplied with the occupational distribution of projected new jobs in the county in which the college is located.

RESPONSIVENESS TO MEETING THE NEEDS OF IMMIGRANTS

Overview of Results

The first thing to note about our data is the high incidence of first-generation immigrants among California community college students. In Chapter 5, we use information on possession of a foreign high school diploma and U.S. citizenship status to estimate that over 30 percent of Latino students and nearly 60 percent of Asian students are first-generation immigrants. At the two-digit level of detail on ethnicity examined in Chapter 6, we find that about 60 percent of students with a national origin of Central America or South America are immigrants. This compares to about 27 percent of Mexicans. Asian students are even more likely to be immigrants than Latinos, and we report in Chapter 6 considerable variation in immigrant status among Asians broken down by ethnicity. Those most likely to be immigrants are students from Southeast Asia (Cambodians, Laotians, and Vietnamese). About three-quarters of Southeast Asian students are immigrants. At the other extreme, immigrants comprise only about one-third of Filipino students.

Our three community college outcome variables include success in transferring to a four-year college, receipt of an AA degree, and total credits earned over a student's community college experience. Chapter 5 reports that Latino students lag behind whites on each of these measures, with a particularly sizable gap observed for transfer rates. Since Latinos attend postsecondary educational institutions at a rate comparable to whites but disproportionately enroll in community colleges, their lower transfer rate is critical in explaining Latinos' lower overall level of educational attainment. On the other hand, Asians exhibit a superior performance in comparison to whites on each of our three outcome variables.

We attempt to account for the observed Latino-white and Asian-white gaps in these community college outcomes by looking for differences in four categories of explanatory variables measured at the individual student level. These categories of explanatory variables include

- background variables, including citizenship status;
- financial need;
- educational goals; and
- community college performance measures.

In addition, we are able to take into account differences in the institutional characteristics of the college attended.

As reported in Chapter 5, factors likely to be helpful in explaining the Latino-white gap in educational outcomes include a lower high school graduation rate (including both U.S. and foreign high school diplomas), a lower average number of courses attempted, less interest in ultimately transferring to a four-year college as opposed to other goals, and poorer academic performance while attending a community college. One factor likely to work in favor of Latinos is their younger average age. At the institutional level, we also observed that community colleges attended by Latinos, in comparison to those attended by whites, tend to be less transfer oriented, to have student bodies that are generally less well prepared for college, and to be located in less affluent communities.

Despite a high proportion of first-generation immigrants, Asian students are at least comparable to white students in terms of many of our explanatory variables. This includes possession of a high school diploma (again including both U.S. and foreign diplomas) and community college progress variables. In addition, Asians tend to be younger, to carry higher average course loads, and to be more interested as entering freshmen in transferring to a four-year college. Community colleges attended by Asian students are closer to UC and CSU campuses and tend to be located in more prosperous communities.

Chapter 5 assesses the importance of these differences in explaining Latino-white and Asian-white gaps in educational outcomes. Looking first at Latinos, we find that controlling for differences across students in our explanatory variables reduced the observed Latino-white gap in transfer rates from about 7.5 percentage points to about 2 percentage points. Smaller observed gaps in AA degree receipt and total credits earned appear to be completely accounted for by our model. The most important category of explanatory variables in terms of explaining observed Latino-white gaps in outcomes is community college progress variables. In turn, we suggest that the relatively slow academic progress of Latino students is due in large part to weaker academic preparation before entering college, a deficiency that often requires taking a higher proportion of basic skills courses while in college.

Breaking down Latinos by ethnic background, our results in Chapter 6 for Mexican students echoed those for all Latinos, a finding that is not surprising since Mexicans are by far the largest category of Latino students. Similarly, we are able to explain most of the observed gaps in transfer rates of Central American and South American students. (Gaps in AA degree receipt and total credits earned are quite small.) It is troubling to note that the transfer rate gap between Mexicans and whites is as large or larger than the gaps observed for Central and South Americans, despite the fact that Mexican students are much less likely to be first-generation immigrants.

Overall, we are less successful in explaining Asian-white gaps in outcome variables, especially for student transfers. Of the observed gap of about 11 percentage points favoring Asians in transfer rates, adjusting for differences in our explanatory variables resulted in a standardized gap of about 8 percentage points. We do a much better job in explaining the Asian-white gap in total credits earned. Factors that make the most difference in reducing the observed gap in credits earned are the "financial need" of students, which we measure by an older age and average course load attempted per semester, and background variables. Asian students tend to be younger than whites and to carry higher average course loads.

Disaggregating Asian students by ethnicity, we are able to substantially explain observed negative transfer gaps (i.e., gaps favoring whites) for Cambodians and Laotians, and observed positive gaps for Filipinos and the Japanese. We do less well in explaining positive, and typically larger, observed gaps for Chinese, Indian, and Korean students. And we are not successful at all in explaining the observed gap of 9 percentage points for the Vietnamese. Note that the Chinese, Filipinos, and Vietnamese are numerically the largest categories of Asian students enrolled in CCCS colleges.

Once we control for student-level variables, we find that differences in college-level characteristics make little difference in explaining either Latino-white or Asian-white gaps in transfer rates. Nevertheless, the importance of institutional characteristics is a question that receives attention in the literature (see, for example, Bailey, et al. 2005), and we pursue this question by estimating individual college fixed effects. Based on evidence of large individual college fixed effects, we explore a hypothesis suggested by Borjas (1999) that the clustering in a college of students of a particular ethnic background might affect that group's overall transfer rate. Our cross-college regression analysis reveals strikingly opposite results for Latinos and Asians. Clustering is found to negatively affect the transfer rate of Latinos, while positively affecting the transfer rate of Asians. We suggest that the Asian result may help in explaining the transfer rate gap favoring Vietnamese students over whites, a gap we are otherwise unable to explain. Immigration statistics indicate that Vietnamese immigrants in California are concentrated in Orange and Santa Clara Counties, and our data suggests that Vietnamese community college students are similarly clustered in a handful of community colleges located in these two counties.

We also isolate on two subpopulations of students likely to be of particular interest to policymakers: first-generation immigrants and high school dropouts. As expected, first-generation immigrant students are heavily Latino and Asian. Among Asians, outcome measures for first-generation immigrant students are found to be roughly the same as those for nonimmigrants. That is, despite disadvantages including lack of proficiency in English and unfamiliarity with American culture, Asian first-generation immigrants do very well in California community colleges. On the other hand, first-generation immigrant Latinos perform at a lower level than nonimmigrant Latinos. In fact, first-generation immigrant Latino students lag behind immigrant students of all other ethnic or racial backgrounds. Leinbach and Bailey (2006) reach the same conclusion for foreign-born Latinos attending the City University of New York—a finding they term both important and disturbing.

Our most striking finding concerning high school dropouts is that, regardless of race or ethnicity, dropouts do much more poorly in terms of our outcome variables than high school graduates. This lack of success is understandable given their individual attributes that include an older age, less interest in transferring, and a lighter average course load with a higher proportion of basic skills courses. As noted in Chapter 5, California community college officials are bracing for an influx of entering students who did not complete high school because they failed the California High School Exit Exam. Our findings do not directly address this concern since they apply to an older population of dropouts than the high school students currently at risk of failing the exit exam. Nevertheless, it is safe to suggest that, should this influx of high school dropouts materialize, community colleges will be required to allocate more resources to teaching basic skills classes. To improve the educational outcomes measured here, in addition, increased effort to retain students through counseling and mentoring programs is likely to be necessary. In what follows, we consider further the design of such programs in the context of assisting Latino students.

Policy Implications

Our results indicated that the low level of community college outcomes for Latino students compared to whites is primarily the result of two factors: 1) poorer performance while attending college, which, in turn, is due to 2) weaker academic background on entering college. California community colleges maintain an open-admissions policy for state residents. Hence, college administrators have little leeway for selectivity in terms of the academic preparation of new students admitted. There is an opportunity, however, for community colleges to improve the academic performance of their Latino students. Indeed, the President's Advisory Commission (2003) on Educational Excellence for Hispanic Americans issues just such a challenge. Five of the six recommendations of the Advisory Commission are specific to K-12 education. The only recommendation that applies directly to postsecondary institutions is that colleges increase their graduation rates by developing retention programs that keep Latino students in school.

What form might these retention programs take? Our cross-college clustering results provide some general guidance for answering this question. As noted, we find that a clustering of Latino students reduces the adjusted transfer rate of Latinos in that college, where the adjusted transfer rate abstracts from differences in individual student characteristics. The clear implication is that retention programs need to be concentrated in colleges with large Latino enrollments. At the federal level, this point was recognized in 1992 legislation that makes Hispanic-serving institutions eligible for special grants and related assistance.

Hispanic-serving institutions are defined as colleges with student enrollment that is 25 percent or more Latino. Thus, predominantly Latino colleges receive equal treatment with traditionally African American colleges and universities.

Also important is the diametrically opposite effect that, for Asians, clustering increases the adjusted transfer rate. In Chapter 6, we consider three explanations for this result. One possibility is that in the absence of family background variables, clustering of Asians captures unobserved differences in family income. This explanation may have traction for Indian, Japanese, and Chinese students, ethnic groups that enjoy remarkably high average family incomes in California. It makes less sense, however, for other Asian groups, including the Vietnamese, for whom average family income falls well below the average for all Asians, which, in turn, slightly exceeds average family income for whites.

A second explanation seems especially applicable to Vietnamese students because of the high proportion that are first-generation immigrants, and, among immigrants, the high proportion that are refugees. The idea is that immigrants who face a high cost of returning to their homelands, such as refugees, have a strong incentive to invest in U.S. schooling. For Asian parents, this explanation appears to be closely related to the "Asian culture" concept by which parents pass on to their children their strong belief that success in the United States depends on educational attainment.

Going beyond Asian culture is a closely related third explanation based on the observation that immigrants often settle in ethnic enclaves. The argument is that close association with unrelated individuals of the same ethnicity imparts to students valuable "ethnic capital" that contributes to their success in the U.S. labor market.

We suggest that the concept of ethnic capital carries over for community college students in the form of a positive peer effect. That is, exposure to students of the same ethnic background who are academically highly motivated encourages a student to set a high standard for him- or herself. Conversely, exposure to peers of the same ethnicity with generally lower levels of motivation may cause a student to lower his or her expectations. This suggests that colleges should offer the kinds of mentoring, academic and career counseling, and peer support programs that might counteract such negative peer effects.

Laden (1999) provides some useful illustrations of programs that support the educational aspirations of Latino students. These include the following:

- Miami-Dade Community College in Florida has developed a system designed to reduce first-generation college students' bewilderment and sense of intimidation. New students are greeted warmly upon arrival, given admissions forms, and invited to sit at a table to fill out forms with the help of a bilingual staff member. Once enrolled, students' attendance and academic progress are monitored, with the goal of heading off problems and maintaining morale and aspirations.

- In California, community colleges including Evergreen College and San Jose City College offer students special articulation transfer contracts with four-year state institutions intended to make the transfer process more seamless.

- Nationally, a number of community colleges maintain transfer centers employing bilingual/bicultural student workers to provide encouragement and tutoring to Latino and other minority students.

- The Puente Project in California, a partnership between the UC system and a number of community colleges, attempts to incorporate Latino students' cultural experiences into the English curriculum during their first year of college.

While these are interesting examples of what might be done, Wassmer, Moore, and Shulock (2004) note, unfortunately, that there is no currently available comprehensive review of community college programs targeted to minority students.

Deil-Amen and Rosenbaum (2003) take an alternative approach—one based on a study of private occupational colleges—to arrive at suggestions for how community colleges might enhance the chances of success of minority and other disadvantaged students.[1] As we have noted, strengths of community colleges including broad program offerings, low cost, and convenient locations allow easy access and broad choice among fields of study. At the same time, it is easy for students, particularly first-generation college students who attended high schools offering little counseling, to run into difficulties. The result is that these students often feel lost, fail to make reasonable progress in their programs, and ultimately drop out. In the words of Deil-Amen and Rosenbaum, nontraditional students' attrition tends to be high because they lack the "social know-how" to succeed in large, impersonal educational institutions.

Private occupational colleges are much more expensive than public community colleges and offer limited choice among programs. Nevertheless, Deil-Amen and Rosenbaum argue that private occupational colleges are able to compete with community colleges by reducing the importance of social know-how. The authors outline four barriers posed by community colleges to students with limited social know-how that appear to be successfully addressed by private occupational colleges. These barriers and the responses of occupational colleges are worth describing in some detail.

1. Bureaucratic hurdles and confusing choices. Community colleges are often large and complex institutions. It is easy for students to be overwhelmed with the available choices, to make poor decisions on the basis of inadequate information, and to find that programs take longer to complete than anticipated. Occupational colleges provide easy access to information on how to enroll and on course requirements for particular majors. Information about financial aid, rather than being the student's own responsibility, is viewed as an integral part of the registration process.

2. The burden of student-initiated assistance. Although community colleges make guidance available, students are typically expected to initiate the process. Nontraditional students often do not know that guidance is available, or, if they do, are reluctant to make an appointment with an advisor. Rather than expecting students to take the initiative to seek out assistance, occupational colleges automatically assign each student to a specific counselor who monitors the student's academic progress.

3. Limited counselor availability, poor advice, and costly mistakes. In comparison to community colleges, occupational colleges invest heavily in counseling services and job placement staff. Easier access to counselors, when combined with fewer

program options to learn about, results in more accurate advice and quicker detection of potentially costly mistakes.

4. Conflicts with outside demands. Students and particularly nontraditional students face outside demands that divert their attention from coursework including financial need, work obligations, and child care crises. Deil-Amen and Rosenbaum suggest that community college faculty and administrators often give the impression that the traditional student model is the ideal, and that if working students struggle with their studies the solution is to reduce hours of work. In contrast, occupational colleges recognize that most students need to work and attempt to make work compatible with students' career goals. This includes blocking courses to reduce commuting time, providing guidance on how to combine education with work, and helping students find career-relevant jobs.

Writing specifically about California community colleges, Shulock and Moore (2007) provide a similar analysis of policies, that while intended to increase access, have the unintended consequence of inhibiting the program completion of increasing under-prepared students.[2] They suggest, in contrast to current CCCS policies, an institutional commitment to student success. Such a commitment would be implemented by proactive and continuous academic counseling, stricter assessment of entering students' basic skills proficiency, requiring students to remedy basic skills deficiencies before enrolling in higher-level classes, a mandatory freshman orientation course, and assisting students to identify program goals and pathways for meeting these goals.

RESPONSIVENESS TO MEETING THE NEEDS OF LOCAL EMPLOYERS

The cross-college examination of the effects of clustering for Latinos and Asians sets the stage for our analysis in Chapter 7 of the quality of matches between the occupational distribution of credits completed supplied by community colleges and the occupational distribution of projected new jobs in counties in which colleges are located. As described earlier in this chapter, we quantify match quality by means of a responsiveness variable (R). Since California community colleges are organized into districts, it is quite possible that labor market responsiveness occurs at the district level, rather than at the individual college level, for colleges in multicampus districts. Hence, we calculate R scores for community college (CC) districts as well as for individual colleges.

For the 106 CCCS colleges we analyze, R scores are found to vary substantially, with the least responsive college receiving a score of 32.4 percent and the most responsive college a score of 81.7 percent. (R scores can range between 1 and 100 percent.) Our analysis reveals that R scores are positively affected by several external constraint measures suggested by Jacobson et al. (2005, Appendix C). These variables include student enrollment, revenue per student, share of local revenue to total revenue, and suburban location. Found not to be important in determining labor market responsiveness is the emphasis a college puts on occupational skills training, which we measure by the share of vocational credits in all credits completed. We also find that it makes little difference whether or not a college is a member of a multicampus CC district.

Our district-level results are distinctly different from these college-level findings. For the 71 districts included in our data set, the R score distribution shifts up in comparison to that for colleges, primarily because of higher scores at the low end of the distribution. Among the external constraint variables, only our measure of local revenue share appears to impact district-level R scores. Holding constant the effects of these external constraints, our major new result is that while membership in a multicampus district had essentially no effect in our college-level relationship, it is strongly positive at the district level, with a coefficient of nearly 6 percentage points.

To draw out the implications of this finding, we argue in Chapter 7 that a simple property of an average would lead to a finding of no effect for the multicampus variable in our district-level relationship. The reasoning is that low-scoring colleges in a multicampus district are likely to have their scores pulled up by other colleges in their district in comparison to low-scoring colleges that comprise their own district. At the same time, R scores for districts that include high-scoring colleges will be drawn down in comparison to high-scoring colleges that are their own district. We thus interpret the finding that multicampus CC districts are more labor market responsive than single-campus districts as suggesting that, at least within some multicampus districts, member colleges choose to specialize in their occupational education curriculums and, furthermore, that these specializations are complementary within districts.

An example provided in Chapter 7 illustrates this point. Serving Alameda County in Northern California, the Peralta CC district includes four colleges. Merritt College and Vista College are found to rank second and third from the bottom, respectively, in terms of their individual R scores (38.3 percent and 38.6 percent, respectively). Within the district, these two colleges are combined with higher-scoring Alameda College (R = 59.9 percent) and Laney College (R = 64.1 percent). But rather than its score lying between those for the low-scoring and higher-scoring member colleges, the Peralta CC district score is 70.5 percent. Not only is the district score considerably above the highest score of any member college, but we noted in Chapter 7 that it is close to the score that would put the Peralta CC district in the top-five districts measured in terms of labor market responsiveness.

Policy Implications

We draw three policy implications from these findings. The first is that a heavy emphasis on occupational skills training as measured by the share of total credits in vocational fields of study does not necessarily carry over to a high score on our measure of labor market responsiveness. Colleges with a low voc-ed credits ratio can be responsive in the occupational skills programs they do offer. A case in point is Santa Barbara City College, which is known within California as a transfer-oriented college and has a voc-ed credits ratio of only about 20 percent. Nevertheless, Santa Barbara City College ranks second among all 106 CCCS colleges in terms of its R score.

The second policy implication relates to our external constraint variables that measure enrollment and the level and source of funding. Not unexpectedly, we find that size and funding affect a college's labor market responsiveness, and that share of local funding enhances responsiveness at the district level. Nevertheless, the fit of our estimated relationships is not such that we can provide accurate predictions of a particular college's or district's responsiveness. We interpret these results as indicating that there is plenty of room for administrators interested in increasing the labor market responsiveness of their colleges to exercise initiative and leadership in seizing upon the opportunities offered in their communities.

A final policy implication involves performance evaluation. The issue is whether performance standards applied uniformly to community colleges, as directed by the federal Workforce Investment Act (WIA) and the Carl D. Perkins Vocational and Technical Education Act (VTEA), are appropriate if colleges differ in their academic missions. In Gill and Leigh (2004), we use college-level data to investigate the extent to which California community colleges differ in their missions. Colleges are found to differ in terms of the mix of their curriculums across transferable, nontransferable voc-ed, and adult basic skills credits, and in terms of the level at which voc-ed courses are taught. The main empirical distinction is between colleges that offer a transfer curriculum specialization and colleges that specialize in nontransferable voc-ed. We conclude that in view of important differences in curriculum offerings, a "one-size-fits-all" evaluation strategy may not be appropriate.

Continuing to focus on community colleges' occupational skills offerings, our analysis in Chapter 7 examines the effectiveness of these offerings as measured by the quality of the matches between the supply of skills colleges provide and the demand for skills by local employers. As already summarized, we find that colleges differ substantially in our measure of match quality. Before labeling low-scoring colleges as non–market responsive, however, we also pointed out that it is important to take into account whether these colleges are members of a multicampus CC district. Based on our evidence, we argue that low-scoring colleges may have low scores because they specialize in the occupational skills training provided, and that when combined with other member colleges that offer complementary specializations, the district is labor market responsive.

QUALIFICATIONS AND OPPORTUNITIES FOR
FURTHER RESEARCH

We conclude our discussion of the labor market responsiveness of community colleges with some final thoughts and a few suggestions for further research.

In terms of meeting the needs of immigrants, our first research question, results presented in Chapters 5 and 6 suggest general guidelines that may be helpful to community colleges for designing programs to increase retention of Latino students. Among Latinos, moreover, such targeted programs appear to be especially important for students of Mexican descent and for colleges with a heavy Mexican enrollment. Earlier in this chapter, we mentioned a few examples of community colleges, including those in California, that offer programs targeting assistance to Latino students. However, more research is urgently needed in the form of more comprehensive surveys of targeted programs. With this information in hand, the next step would be to proceed with a formal evaluation of the different types of programs. The barriers to a successful community college experience identified by Deil-Amen and Rosenbaum (2003) could serve as a useful standard against which to evaluate these programs.

To answer Research Question 2, we argue in Chapter 7 that matching a community college's supply of skills to local employers' demand for skilled workers represents a simple and intuitive method for assessing the effectiveness of a college's occupational skills training programs. As emphasized, the labor demand measure we use is projected employment across major occupational categories measured at the county level. On the supply side, we measure a college's distribution of vocational credits completed classified by the same occupational codes. We view our methodology as a reasonable first approach to providing a quantitative measure of labor market effectiveness that allows individual colleges, and districts, in a state community college system to be directly compared. Nevertheless, there is the possibility that a college that is actually responsive to local employers' needs might receive a low R score.

An important issue is the use of counties to represent the geographical dimension of the local labor market. While we would argue that counties represent a reasonable approximation of the labor market relevant to students enrolled in most California community colleges, there are some counties for which this is not likely to be the case. A leading example is Los Angeles County, which has a gross domestic product exceeding that of many small nations. The question is whether a county as large and complex as Los Angeles County really represents the relevant local labor market for a particular community college, or even a community college district, located in the county?

To push this issue one step further, consider the case of a community college that is filling a market "niche" by supplying trained workers to one or a handful of local employers who offer relatively few, but high-paying, jobs. At the level of aggregation we use, the few jobs described in this example are unlikely to be reflected in the occupational distribution of projected job opportunities measured at the county level. Yet, this college might reasonably be considered as labor market responsive.

With the Los Angeles County case and the example of a community college that supplies a particular market niche, we are suggesting that it is important to know how the college itself defines its market, which in turn is likely to depend on how it prioritizes its missions. This kind of information is likely to be accessed only through site visits, indicating the desirability of a case study approach to complement the empirically based approach we implement.

One final thought relates to the relationship between Research Questions 1 and 2. We indicate in Chapter 1 that the two questions are not independent. Yet our analysis in Chapters 5 and 6 does not directly address the question of whether community college students who are current or recent immigrants are obtaining the occupational skills they need to qualify for jobs in the local labor market. Instead, we examine the effect of attending a community college on a broader set of educational outcomes (student transfers, AA degree receipt, and total credits earned) that are known to have positive labor market payoffs. Our analysis in Chapter 7, similarly, does not examine whether the occupational training received by current or recent immigrants attending a community college is a good match for new jobs opening up in the local labor market. Rather, we calculate R scores for colleges using data for all their students.

A few of the results we report in Chapters 5, 6, and 7 give a hint of what one might expect to find for the overlap between our Research Questions 1 and 2. For example, we find in Chapter 7 that colleges that are the most market responsive are often located in suburban areas in Orange County and the San Francisco Bay Peninsula. In Chapters 5 and 6, in turn, we report that Asian and especially Vietnamese immigrants are concentrated in the same suburban areas. The suggestion is that community colleges disproportionately attended by Asian immigrants are responsive to changing local labor market conditions.

Nevertheless, we believe that a direct examination of the intersection between our two research questions would be fruitful. As one example, future research might narrow the scope of our second research question to focus on particular groups of students, say, first-generation Mexican and Asian immigrants, while widening the outcome variables considered in answering Question 1 to include training appropriate to job opportunities in the local labor market. Hence, an interesting research question emerges: Do community colleges provide occupational training to new Mexican and Asian immigrants that gives them the skills necessary to compete in the local economy? It is our hope that the empirical research presented in this monograph will stimulate more questions and additional research that will further illuminate the critical role of community colleges in helping nontraditional students, such as first-generation immigrants, adjust to the demands of the U.S. labor market.

Notes

1. The authors make it clear that their study is based on a restricted, nonrandom set of private occupational colleges. Two criteria were imposed in selecting these occupational colleges. First, selected institutions offer accredited two-year degrees in applied programs such as business, accounting, computer information systems, electronics, and medical technology. This characteristic makes them comparable to community colleges. Second, selected occupational colleges have low loan default rates and, according to the authors, are considered to offer some of the best applied programs available.

2. The five policy barriers identified by Shulock and Moore (2007) are 1) funding based on course enrollment reported early in the semester or quarter; 2) limits on expenditures on staff providing essential student services including advising; 3) restrictions on hiring that limit colleges' flexibility in offering courses, especially occupational training and basic skills courses; 4) student fee policies that encour-

age students to enroll in classes without much forethought and deprive colleges of needed revenue; and 5) an institutional philosophy that "students have the right to fail."

Appendix A
Data Sources

The Chancellor's Office of the California Community College System (CCCS) made available to us complete student records for four cohorts of first-time-freshmen (FTF) students who enrolled at any CCCS campus in fall 1993 through fall 1996. We chose to analyze the 1996 FTF cohort. The academic progress of each cohort of students is followed for six years. Thus, first-time freshmen included in the 1996 cohort are followed from their initial enrollment in fall 1996 through 2002.

Four data files are available for each cohort:

1) cohort file,

2) awards file,

3) transfer file, and

4) enrollment file.

Files can be linked by social security number or, in a small number of cases, another student identifier. The first section of this appendix describes the steps we went through to merge the four student data files. Since we can identify the college each student initially attended, we are able to append to this data set a number of college-level variables of interest. The second section of the appendix describes the merger of our student records with these college-level variables.

INDIVIDUAL STUDENT DATA FILES

The Cohort File

This file includes basic demographic information for each student such as age at first enrollment, gender, race or ethnicity, citizenship, high school graduation status, and community college attended. A complicating factor is the existence of up to six duplicate observations for the same student as identified by his or her social security number. The problem is that the information on duplicate observations is not necessarily the same. For example, we observe for the same student different first colleges attended. Conversations with Myra

Hoffman in the Chancellor's Office indicated that the likely explanation of duplicate observations is sporadic enrollment behavior. That is, some students enroll, then drop out, then enroll again, possibly at another college, and then drop out again.

Since we do not know which observation is correct for a particular individual, we delete all students for whom there are duplicate observations. We lose 7,957 students by imposing this restriction.

The Awards File

The awards file includes information on degrees earned, certificates (including hours required for the award), date of award, community college of award, and TOP code for award. This file is organized by award, with up to 15 awards allowed for each student. Viewed as an Excel spreadsheet, that is, for each student there are 15 rows of data, one row for each possible award. To make the file readable in the statistical analysis program SAS, we transposed the award rows into columns. Now each row contains information for a single person. But since few students have more than one award (either an AA degree or a certificate), allowing the maximum 15 columns for every student means that the transposed data file contains a large number of empty cells. To make the data file more manageable, we limit individual students to four awards. There are a total of 41,505 students in the 1996 cohort included in the awards file. The restriction we impose results in the loss of just 206 individuals for whom five or more awards are reported.

The Transfer File

This file includes data for students who transferred to a two-year or four-year institution on the transfer destination college, the state in which the college is located, whether the college is public or private, and the date of transfer. Up to seven transfer events are reported for each student. A total of 59,443 students in the 1996 cohort transferred during the six-year observation period. We limit the number of transfer events to six, which results in the loss of three individuals.

The Enrollment File

Finally, the enrollment file is organized by the number of courses that students attempted and completed. Courses are described by whether they are taken for credit, their TOP code, whether they are transferable, and letter grade earned. Up to 187 courses for each student are included in the data file. Since it takes only about 20 courses to earn an AA degree, we again faced the problem of a large number of empty cells when the file is transposed. To avoid retaining columns that contain information for only a few respondents, we limit the number of courses to 70. This restriction results in the loss of 1,448 respondents for whom information on more than 70 courses is reported.

Merging across Data Files

After imposing these restrictions on the individual data files, we proceeded to merge the data for the 1996 FTF cohort across all four files. The resulting merged data set includes 359,400 students. With the merged data set in hand, one more problem to be dealt with is the circumstance in which data exist for a student in one file but not another. We address this problem by omitting from our merged data set students for whom no information is reported in a particular data file. The data files for which this problem arises are the Enrollment File and the Cohort File. When we omit all respondents for whom no enrollment information is reported, the merged data set drops by 15,666 individuals to 343,734 students. Omitting all respondents for whom we have no cohort information, the merged data set drops by another 7,768 individuals to 335,966 students.

Descriptive statistics for the individual student variables included in our data extract appear in Tables A.1 and A.2. Table A.1 describes community college outcome variables and measures of student performance while attending a community college. Table A.2 relates to variables measuring students' demographic characteristics, educational goals, and educational backgrounds.

APPENDING COLLEGE-LEVEL VARIABLES

Using the college identifier indicating the college at which each student initially enrolled, we appended to the merged student data set several variables measuring college-level characteristics. The 1996 FTF data set includes students who attended any one of 108 CCCS colleges. As described in Chapter 7, however, usable data are not available for Copper Mountain Community College and Santiago Canyon College. Hence, we include in our data extract college-level characteristics for 106 colleges. In addition, data for the 1996 student cohort includes information for 351 students enrolled at Los Angeles Instructional Television (ITV). Los Angeles ITV is not commonly included as a member of the CCCS. We consequently omitted data for these 351 Los Angeles ITV students. After merging our student records for the 1996 cohort

Table A.1 Outcome and Performance Variable Definitions and Descriptive Statistics for the 1996 CCCS Student Cohort

Student-level variable	Mean	Minimum	Maximum
One or more AA or AS degrees earned	0.090	0.0	1.0
Earned a certificate (first award only)			
Required 6–17 semester units	0.003	0.0	1.0
Required 18–29 semester units	0.009	0.0	1.0
Required 30–59 semester units	0.012	0.0	1.0
Required 60 or more semester units	0.002	0.0	1.0
Other certificate	0.004	0.0	1.0
Number of transferable courses			
Transferable to both UC and CSU	7.7	0.0	64.0
Transferable to CSU only	2.8	0.0	57.0
Not transferable	4.5	0.0	65.0
Number of courses taken for credit, degree applicable			
Taken for credit, degree applicable	12.5	0.0	70.0
Taken for credit, not degree applicable	1.6	0.0	62.0
Noncredit	0.9	0.0	60.0
Number of basic skills courses taken			
Precollegiate level	1.1	0.0	51.0
Not precollegiate level	0.3	0.0	53.0
Not basic skills	13.6	0.0	70.0
GPA ($N = 286,384$)[a]	2.26	0.0	4.0
Number of credits attempted	40.1	0.0	284.0
Number of credits earned	26.4	0.0	218.0
Transferred to a 4-year or 2-year college			
Ever transferred to a 4-year college	0.143	0.0	1.0
Ever transferred to a 2-year college	0.025	0.0	1.0

NOTE: $N = 335,966$.

[a] Omits students who took only nongraded courses.

with our college-level variables, our data extract includes information for a total of 335,615 students.

Table A.3 reports summary statistics for the college-level variables included in our data extract. The Academic Preparation Index (API) measuring standardized test scores for college freshmen is found in Office of Planning, Research, and Grants Development (2002). The remaining college-level variables are taken from Gill and Leigh (2004).

Table A.2 Demographic Characteristics, Educational Goals, and Educational Background Variable Definitions and Descriptive Statistics for the 1996 CCCS Student Cohort

Student-level variable	Mean (%)
Gender	
Male	48.5
Female	51.0
Other	0.5
Race/ethnicity (one-digit)	
Hispanic	26.6
White	40.0
Asian	10.5
Black	9.4
Filipino	3.0
American Indian	1.4
Other nonwhite	1.8
Pacific Islander	0.7
Unknown	4.6
Declined to state	2.0
Age at first term attended	
Less than 18	6.3
18–19	38.3
20–22	14.7
23–29	16.0
30–39	13.4
40–49	7.1
50–59	2.6
60 and older	1.4
Missing	0.2
High school background	
No high school degree and no longer enrolled	10.2
Special admittance (currently in K-12)	0.3
Currently enrolled in an adult school	1.3
High school diploma	70.1
Passed GED	5.8
California high school proficiency certificate	1.3
Foreign secondary school diploma	6.6
Unknown or unreported	4.5

(continued)

Table A.2 (continued)

Student-level variable	Mean (%)
Citizenship status	
U.S. citizen	79.4
Permanent resident	15.1
Temporary resident	0.5
Refugee/asylee	0.9
Student visa (F1 or M1 visa)	1.3
Other status	0.9
Unknown status	1.8
Financial aid	
Federal need based	2.9
Other need based	1.5
Federal nonneed based	0.1
Scholarship	0.3
Other financial aid	0.1
No financial aid	95.1
Disability status	
No disability	97.6
Mobility impaired	0.3
Visually impaired	0.1
Hearing impaired	0.1
Speech/language impaired	0.0
Delayed learner	0.2
Brain injury	0.2
Learning disabled	0.9
Psychologically disabled	0.2
Other disability	0.5
Educational goal uninformed by counseling	
Transfer with AA degree	25.3
Transfer without AA degree	8.5
AA degree without planning to transfer	5.0
Vocational degree without planning to transfer	2.8
Vocational certificate without planning to transfer	3.6
Discover career	4.7
New career	8.4
Advance career	5.2
Maintain certificate/license	1.4

Table A.2 (continued)

Student-level variable	Mean (%)
Educational development	5.3
Basic skills	3.5
Obtain credits for a GED	1.7
Undecided	20.9
Uncollected or unreported	3.7
Lacks proficiency in English	
Took ESL course	7.1
Needs ESL course	0.4
No need for ESL course	92.5
Academic standing	
Good	89.6
Progress probation	3.1
Academic probation	5.1
Progress and academic probation	0.7
Progress dismissal	0.1
Academic dismissal	0.2
Progress and academic dismissal	0.0
Unknown	1.3
Not available	—

NOTE: N = 335,966.

Table A.3 College-Level Variable Definitions and Descriptive Statistics for the 1996 CCCS Student Cohort

College-level variable	Mean	Minimum	Maximum
Academic Preparation Index	47.7	30.8	57.7
Transfer credits/all credits	0.75	0.19	0.92
Distance to nearest UC (in miles)	36.3	1.7	282.5
Distance to nearest CSU (in miles)	18.3	1.5	178.2
Median HH income ($,000)	50.7	21.9	173.6
Percent of population age 25+ with BA degree	27.8	5.4	78.1

NOTE: N = 335,615.

References

Alfonso, Mariana. 2006. "The Educational Attainment of Hispanics in Sub-baccalaureate Education." Paper based on a study prepared for the Community Colleges and Latino Educational Opportunity Roundtable, October 11, 2003, sponsored by the Civil Rights Project at Harvard University, Cambridge, MA.

Alfonso, Mariana, Thomas R. Bailey, and Marc Scott. 2005. "The Educational Outcomes of Occupational Sub-baccalaureate Students: Evidence from the 1990s." *Economics of Education Review* 24(2): 197–212.

Anderson, Stuart. 2004. "The Multiplier Effect." *International Educator* (Summer): 14–21.

Antecol, Heather, and Kelly Bedard. 2002. "The Relative Earnings of Young Mexican, Black, and White Women." *Industrial and Labor Relations Review* 56(1): 122–135.

———. 2004. "The Racial Wage Gap: The Importance of Labor Force Attachment Differences across Black, Mexican, and White Men." *Journal of Human Resources* 39(2): 564–583.

Bailey, Thomas, Juan C. Calcagno, Davis Jenkins, Gregory Kienzl, and Timothy Leinbach. 2005. "Community College Student Success: What Institutional Characteristics Make a Difference?" Unpublished manuscript. New York: Columbia University, Community College Research Center.

Bailey, Thomas, Juan C. Calcagno, Davis Jenkins, Timothy Leinbach, and Gregory Kienzl. 2006. "Is Student-Right-to-Know All You Should Know? An Analysis of Community College Graduation Rates." *Research in Higher Education* 47(5): 491–519.

Bailey, Thomas, and Elliot Weininger. 2002. "Performance, Graduation, and Transfer of Immigrants and Natives in City University of New York Community Colleges." CCRC Working Paper no. 2. New York: Columbia University, Community College Research Center.

Baldassare, Mark. 2006. *California's Future: In Your Hands*. San Francisco: Public Policy Institute of California.

Borjas, George J. 1982. "The Earnings of Male Hispanic Immigrants in the United States." *Industrial and Labor Relations Review* 35(3): 343–353.

———. 1987. "Self-Selection and the Earnings of Immigrants." *American Economic Review* 77(4): 531–553.

———. 1995. "Ethnicity, Neighborhoods, and Human-Capital Externalities." *American Economic Review* 85(3): 365–390.

———. 1999. *Heaven's Door: Immigration Policy and the American Economy*. Princeton, NJ: Princeton University Press.

Bradburn, Ellen M., and David G. Hurst. 2001. "Community College Transfer Rates to 4-Year Institutions Using Alternative Definitions of Transfer." *Education Statistics Quarterly* 3(3): 119–125.

California Department of Finance. n.d. *They Came to California: Legal Immigration in 2000.* Report by the California Department of Finance, Demographic Research Unit, Sacramento, CA.

California Postsecondary Education Commission. 2006. "On-Line Data." http://www.cpec.ca.gov (accessed April 18, 2006).

Carlton, Jim. 2005. "Judgment Day: In Special Election, California Governor Faces Tough Battle." *Wall Street Journal*, November 5, A:1.

Chancellor's Office. 2002. *Transfer Capacity and Readiness in the California Community Colleges.* Report by the California Community College System, Sacramento, CA.

———. 2005. *Fee Policy Framework: Board of Governors Study Session.* Report by the California Community College System, Sacramento, CA.

———. n.d. *Fiscal Data Abstract, 2001–02.* Report by the California Community College System, Fiscal Standards and Information Section, Sacramento, CA.

Chiswick, Barry R. 1983. "An Analysis of the Earnings and Employment of Asian-American Men." *Journal of Labor Economics* 1(2): 197–214.

Cohen, Arthur M., and Florence B. Brawer. 1996. *The American Community College.* 3rd ed. San Francisco: Jossey-Bass.

Cortes, Kalena E. 2004. "Are Refugees Different from Economic Immigrants? Some Empirical Evidence on the Heterogeneity of Immigrant Groups in the United States." *Review of Economics and Statistics* 86(2): 465–480.

Deil-Amen, Regina, and James E. Rosenbaum. 2003. "The Social Prerequisites of Success: Can College Structure Reduce the Need for Social Know-How?" *The Annals of the American Academy of Political and Social Science* 586(1): 120–143.

Dougherty, Kevin J. 2003. "The Uneven Distribution of Employee Training by Community Colleges: Description and Explanation." *The Annals of the American Academy of Political and Social Science* 586(1): 62–91.

Douglass, John A. 2000. *The California Idea and American Higher Education: 1850 to the 1960 Master Plan.* Stanford, CA: Stanford University Press.

Ehrenberg, Ronald G., and Christopher L. Smith. 2004. "Analyzing the Success of Student Transitions from 2- to 4-Year Institutions within a State." *Economics of Education Review* 23(1): 11–28.

Employment Development Department. 2005. "Job Outlook for California Community College Occupational Education Programs." Sacramento, CA: Employment Development Department. http://www.calmis.ca.gov (accessed September 22, 2005).

Fry, Richard. 2002. *Latinos in Higher Education: Many Enroll, Too Few Graduate.* Washington, DC: Pew Hispanic Center.

Funkhouser, Edward, and Stephen J. Trejo. 1995. "The Labor Market Skills of Recent Male Immigrants: Evidence From the Current Population Survey." *Industrial and Labor Relations Review* 48(4): 792–811.

Ganderton, Philip T., and Richard Santos. 1995. "Hispanic College Attendance and Completion: Evidence from the High School and Beyond Surveys." *Economics of Education Review* 14(1): 35–46.

Gill, Andrew M., and Duane E. Leigh. 2003. "Do the Returns to Community College Differ between Academic and Vocational Programs?" *Journal of Human Resources* 38(1): 134–155.

———. 2004. *Evaluating Academic Programs in California's Community Colleges.* San Francisco: Public Policy Institute of California.

Gonzales, Arturo, and Michael J. Hilmer. Forthcoming. "The Role of Two-Year Colleges in the Improving Situation of Hispanic Postsecondary Education." *Economics of Education Review.*

Grubb, W. Norton. 1996. *Working In the Middle: Strengthening Education and Training for the Mid-Skilled Labor Force.* San Francisco: Jossey-Bass.

Harmon, Robert, and Keith MacAllum. 2003. *Documented Characteristics of Labor Market–Responsive Community Colleges and a Review of Supporting Literature.* Washington, DC: U.S. Department of Education, Office of Vocational and Adult Education.

Hwang, Suein. 2005: "The New White Flight." *Wall Street Journal*, November 19, A:1.

Isbell, Kellie, John Trutko, and Burt S. Barnow. 2000. "Customized Training for Employers: Training People for Jobs that Exist and Employers Who Want to Hire Them." In *Improving the Odds: Increasing the Effectiveness of Publicly Funded Training,* Burt S. Barnow and Christopher T. King, eds. Washington, DC: Urban Institute Press, pp. 209–225.

Jacobson, Louis, Robert J. LaLonde, and Daniel Sullivan. 2005a. "The Impact of Community College Retraining on Older Displaced Workers: Should We Teach Old Dogs New Tricks?" *Industrial and Labor Relations Review* 58(3): 398–415.

———. 2005b. "Estimating the Returns to Community College Schooling for Displaced Workers." *Journal of Econometrics* 125(1–2): 271–304.

Jacobson, Louis, Regina Yudd, Lloyd Feldman, and Ian Petta. 2005. *The 21st-Century Community College: A Strategic Guide for Maximizing Labor Market Responsiveness, Research Appendices.* Washington, DC: U.S. Department of Education, Office of Vocational and Adult Education.

Kane, Thomas J., and Cecilia Elena Rouse. 1995. "Labor-Market Returns to Two- and Four-Year College." *American Economic Review* 85(3): 600–614.

————. 1999. "The Community College: Educating Students at the Margin between College and Work." *Journal of Economic Perspectives* 13(1): 63–84.

Krueger, Alan, and Cecilia Elena Rouse. 1998. "The Effect of Workplace Education on Earnings, Turnover, and Job Performance." *Journal of Labor Economics* 16(1): 61–94.

Laden, Berta V. 1999. "Two-Year Hispanic-Serving Colleges." In *Two-Year Colleges for Women and Minorities: Enabling Access to the Baccalaureate,* Barbara K. Townsend, ed. New York: Falmer Press, pp. 151–194.

Lazear, Edward P. 2005. "Mexican Assimilation in the United States." Unpublished manuscript. Palo Alto, CA: Graduate School of Business, Stanford University.

Leigh, Duane E., and Andrew M. Gill. 1997. "Labor Market Returns to Community Colleges: Evidence for Returning Adults." *Journal of Human Resources* 32(4): 334–353.

————. 2001. "Adults Returning to School—Payoffs from Studying at a Community College." In *Working Time in Comparative Perspective. Vol. 2, Life-Cycle Working Time and Nonstandard Work,* Susan Houseman and Alice Nakamura, eds. Kalamazoo, MI: W.E. Upjohn Institute for Employment Research, pp. 75–97.

————. 2003. "Do Community Colleges Really Divert Students from Earning Bachelor's Degrees?" *Economics of Education Review* 22(11): 23–30.

————. 2004. "The Effect of Community Colleges on Changing Students' Educational Aspirations." *Economics of Education Review* 23(1): 95–102.

Leinbach, D. Timothy, and Thomas R. Bailey. 2006. "Access and Achievement of Hispanics and Hispanic Immigrants in the Colleges of the City University of New York." Paper based on a study prepared for the Community Colleges and Latino Educational Opportunity Roundtable, October 11, 2003, sponsored by the Civil Rights Project at Harvard University, Cambridge, MA.

MacAllum, Keith, and Karla Yoder. 2004. *The 21st-Century Community College: A Strategic Guide to Maximizing Labor Market Responsiveness.* 3 vols. Washington, DC: U.S. Department of Education, Office of Vocational and Adult Education.

Mosisa, Abraham T. 2002. "The Role of Foreign-Born Workers in the U.S. Economy." *Monthly Labor Review* 125(5): 3–14.

Mueser, Peter, Kenneth R. Troske, and Alexey Gorislavsky. 2003. "Using State Administrative Data to Measure Program Performance." IZA discussion paper no. 786. Bonn, Germany: Institute for the Study of Labor.

Murphy, Patrick J. 2004. *Financing California's Community Colleges.* San Francisco: Public Policy Institute of California.

National Center for Education Statistics. 2002. *Digest of Education Statistics, 2001.* Washington, DC: U.S. Department of Education.

Oaxaca, Ronald L. 1973. "Male-Female Wage Differentials in Urban Labor Markets." *International Economic Review* 14(3): 693–709.

Office of Planning, Research, and Grants Development, San Joaquin Delta College. 2002. "Community College Transfer Rates: A Re-Analysis of Statewide Data." Stockton, CA: San Joaquin Delta College. http://www.deltacollege.edu/div/planning/TRANSFERREPORT.pdf (accessed Feb 14, 2007).

Osterman, Paul, and Rosemary Batt. 1993. "Employer-Centered Training for International Competitiveness: Lessons from State Programs." *Journal of Policy Analysis and Management* 12(3): 456–477.

Paddock, Richard C. 2006. "Report Faults Community Colleges." *Los Angeles Times*, November 17, B:5. http://www.latimes.com/news/local/la-me-college17nov17,1,1905199.story?coll=la-headlines-california (accessed March 8, 2007).

President's Advisory Commission. 2003. *From Risk to Opportunity: Fulfilling the Educational Needs of Hispanic Americans in the 21st Century.* Final Report of the President's Advisory Commission on Educational Excellence for Hispanic Americans. Washington, DC: President's Advisory Commission on Educational Excellence for Hispanic Americans.

Rand California. 2003. *Business and Economic Statistics: Gross State Product Statistics.* http://ca.rand.org/stats/economics/gsp.html (accessed January 16, 2007).

Reimers, Cordelia W. 1983. "Labor Market Discrimination against Hispanic and Black Men." *Review of Economics and Statistics* 65(4): 570–579.

Rose, Peter I. 1985. "Asian Americans: From Pariahs to Paragons." In *Clamor At the Gates: The New American Immigration,* Nathan Glazer, ed. San Francisco: ICS Press, pp. 181–212.

Rouse, Cecilia Elena. 1995. "Democratization or Diversion? The Effect of Community Colleges on Educational Attainment." *Journal of Business and Economic Statistics* 13(2): 217–224.

Sengupta, Ria, and Christopher Jepsen. 2006. "California's Community College Students." *California Counts: Population Trends and Profiles* 8(2): 1–23.

Shulock, Nancy, and Colleen Moore. 2007. *Rules of the Game: How State Policy Creates Barriers to Degree Completion and Impedes Student Success in the California Community Colleges.* Sacramento, CA: California State University, Sacramento, Institute for Higher Education Leadership and Policy.

Surette, Brian J. 2001. "Transfer from Two-Year to Four-Year College: An Analysis of Gender Differences." *Economics of Education Review* 20(2): 151–163.

Trejo, Stephen J. 1997. "Why Do Mexican Americans Earn Low Wages?" *Journal of Political Economy* 105(6): 1235–1268.

U.S. Census Bureau. 2000. *American FactFinder Fact Sheet: Census 2000 Demographic Profile Highlights.* http://www.factfinder.census.gov/servlet/ SAFFFacts?_even=&geo_id=01000US&_geoContext=01000US&_street =&_county=&_cityTown=&_state=&_zip=&_lang=en&_sse=on &ActiveGeoDiv=&_useEV=petxt=fph&pgs|=010&_submenuId =factsheet_0&ds_name=ACS_2005_SAFF&_ci_nbr=null&qr_name =null&reg=&_keywork=&_industry= (accessed April 9, 2007).

U.S. Citizenship and Immigration Services. 2002. *Immigration Information.* "Supplemental Tables." No longer available after site was redesigned in October 2006. Comparable immigration statistics are currently available at https://www.dhs.gov/ximgtn/statistics/publications/LPR06.shtm (accessed June 4, 2007).

Wassmer, Robert, Colleen Moore, and Nancy Shulock. 2004. "Effect of Racial/Ethnic Composition on Transfer Rates in Community Colleges: Implications for Policy and Practice." *Research in Higher Education* 45(6): 651–672.

Zeng, Zeng, and Yu Xie. 2004. "Asian Americans' Earnings Disadvantage Reexamined: The Role of Place of Education." *American Journal of Sociology* 109(5): 1075–1108.

Zhou, Min, and Carl L. Bankston III. 1998. *Growing Up American: How Vietnamese Children Adapt to Life in the United States.* New York: Russell Sage Foundation.

The Authors

Duane E. Leigh is professor emeritus of economics at Washington State University, Pullman. He was economics department chair from 1994 to 2003, and he has held teaching and research appointments at the University of Wisconsin–Madison and the University of Virginia. Since the mid-1980s, his research has focused on the operation and labor market effects of training programs directed toward displaced workers and female welfare recipients. He is the author of three earlier monographs published by the Upjohn Institute—*Assisting Displaced Workers: Do the States Have a Better Idea?* (1989); *Does Training Work for Displaced Workers? A Survey of Existing Evidence* (1990); and *Assisting Workers Displaced by Structural Change: An International Perspective* (1995). He and Dr. Gill recently completed a monograph for the Public Policy Institute of California titled *Evaluating Academic Programs in California's Community Colleges*. Dr. Leigh and his wife currently reside in Newberg, Oregon.

Andrew Gill is professor of economics at California State University, Fullerton, specializing in labor economics and econometrics. His research explores human capital issues, gender and racial discrimination, and occupational wage differentials. He has been invited to speak to institutional researchers and community college administrators about avenues for future research on community college issues. Professor Gill served as a Content Expert for the U.S. Department of Education, Institute of Education Sciences, and was a review panelist for the District Level Accountability Framework for California Community Colleges. He also is currently coeditor for the journal *Contemporary Economic Policy*.

Index

The italic letters *n* and *t* following a page number indicate that the subject information of the heading is within a note or table on that page.

About the Institute

The W.E. Upjohn Institute for Employment Research is a nonprofit research organization devoted to finding and promoting solutions to employment-related problems at the national, state, and local levels. It is an activity of the W.E. Upjohn Unemployment Trustee Corporation, which was established in 1932 to administer a fund set aside by Dr. W.E. Upjohn, founder of the Upjohn Company, to seek ways to counteract the loss of employment income during economic downturns.

The Institute is funded largely by income from the W.E. Upjohn Unemployment Trust, supplemented by outside grants, contracts, and sales of publications. Activities of the Institute comprise the following elements: 1) a research program conducted by a resident staff of professional social scientists; 2) a competitive grant program, which expands and complements the internal research program by providing financial support to researchers outside the Institute; 3) a publications program, which provides the major vehicle for disseminating the research of staff and grantees, as well as other selected works in the field; and 4) an Employment Management Services division, which manages most of the publicly funded employment and training programs in the local area.

The broad objectives of the Institute's research, grant, and publication programs are to 1) promote scholarship and experimentation on issues of public and private employment and unemployment policy, and 2) make knowledge and scholarship relevant and useful to policymakers in their pursuit of solutions to employment and unemployment problems.

Current areas of concentration for these programs include causes, consequences, and measures to alleviate unemployment; social insurance and income maintenance programs; compensation; workforce quality; work arrangements; family labor issues; labor-management relations; and regional economic development and local labor markets.